MW00778706

A Cowboy Goes to War

by

Ralph McDougal

A Cowboy
Goes to War

ISBN-13: 978-0-9905724-1-1
Library of Congress Control Number: 2014913199
Technical Editor: Nelson Ottenhausen
Managing Editor: Dari Bradley
Senior Editor: Doris Littlefield
Cover photo and graphics: Ralph McDougal & Dari Bradley

Published by Patriot Media, Inc.
Publishing America's Patriots
P.O. Box 5414
Niceville, FL 32578
United States of America
patriotmediainc.com

Ralph with his playmates.

INTRODUCTION

"The ranch" has always been a magical place for me. Grandpa Hamp laughed, riveted us with stories about the old days, and welcomed the whole town to come out and ride. Grandma Mamie, quiet and brilliant, could prepare dinner for fifty unexpected guests (I've watched her!). They spawned 7 children; Ralph was #5 and my mother Nettie was #2. Mother brought me up on her stories, but regretfully they were never written down. After getting acquainted with my fabled uncle Ralph when he was 87, I discovered his stories linked his fascinating childhood with an illustrious military career.

"Can I write this stuff down?" I asked him.

He shrugged. "Sure."

As he began to relive the tales, more were resurrected, and his memory amazed me. "You can check this out on Internet," he'd say. I was hooked. The long-term life of our family illustrates the American Dream—lessons in hard work, loss, personal initiative, survival, and war. It teaches how to get along, how things work, the value of a positive perspective … and says if you're right then go for it! It shows over time the ultimate triumph of God's goodness.

Best of all, Ralph and his lovely wife Delah continue to relish interesting and active lives! They travel, raise money for an orphanage, support each other, and make new friends. It's a vibrant way to live. Welcome to our family!

Dr. Sharon Anderson

FOREWORD

Ralph McDougal's humorous and reflective account of pre, during, and post WWII is powerful storytelling. The chapters are filled with folklore (water witching), folk tales and memories of compelling prose and poetry. This book is written in a manner that made easy and addictive reading.

This cowboy who goes to war has a very strong identity with other cowboys from various counties across the thirty-one which comprised the State of New Mexico during the late thirties and early forties.

I could easily identify with some of the places he was raised and later traveled; I also was there in about the same time-frame … Tres Hermanas, the Floridas, Las Cruces, Mesilla, El Paso, and his duty stations in Columbus, Ohio; Kansas City Missouri; Belen, New Mexico; Albuquerque, NM, at Kirtland Air Force Base. As well as Japan.

If only the Albuquerque journalist Ernie Pyle were still here, he'd have kept us current on our cowboys who went to war in his usual commentary on the stuff cowboys are made of and their contribution to the greatest generation that is so evident in this book. I am certain this autobiography would be given a rave review by Ernie Pyle.

The choices of lifestyle which Ralph McDougal made and his commitment to his family, his neighbors, his state and his nation will help explain the achievements of his generation. Even today as we watch the news and see the results of drone bombardment of ISIS targets in Iraq, we see and understand the contributions Major McDougal made post WWII.

Childhood stories included in this autobiography wind through various regions across the state of New Mexico—Logan, Roy, Luna, Tucumcari, Nara Visa, and the eastern part of the State, including Curry, Lea, Roosevelt, and Chavez counties and to the west McKinley county. Readers will enjoy and identify with life on a ranch, living in dugouts and the pioneer existence that he and his forebears had. I think this will become an important book for New Mexico. I closed this book with the thought: *Major McDougal has great style and A Cowboy Goes to War is enjoyable reading.*

Thank you for your service, Mr. McDougal, to your family, your county, your state, and to your nation.

I salute you, Major.

Nolan Craig
Member: USS *Frank E. Evans* DD 754 Association

A Cowboy Goes to War

Chapter 1

Growing Up on the Ranch

This is my memoir as I recall it. I'm going back 80-plus years and trying to remember…

Whoopee! It was 1925 and Dad finally had a boy after four girls. Well, he was expecting a big, strong boy to help him on the ranch—and what did he get? A scrawny little towheaded runt. I think he pretty much ignored me until I was nine years old and then decided to do the best he could with what he had. So he took me in hand and taught me about the Lord God, Jesus Christ, the Holy Spirit, and the Bible. He also taught me how to work, how to take responsibility, how to figure things out, and to be right and stand by the truth. Oh my—how that has served me. I think it served me better than it did him.

Let's start with my first memory. I had a fantastic childhood. I was two years old and we were coming home about dusk in the evening in a Model T touring car and as we got close we could see that our house was on fire. My dad parked the car out a little ways from the fire and Mom sat me down on the other side of the car. The picture in my mind is watching the house burn by looking under that Model T Ford.

My next memory is hauling a big cottonwood tree in the back seat of the Model T and planting it in the front yard. The tree was 8' tall and 6-8" in diameter because it took two grown men to get it out of the old Model T (family car at the time). The tree had forked and one of the forks had a fork—but one of the original forks didn't live and left a stump. Years later we set our bed in that tree and the stump supported our bed so it didn't throw us out 12–15 feet up.

Dad traded for an old two-room schoolhouse over on the highway, and he had the ground all ready where he was going to put it. Well, it was a great place to drive my pedal-in-car. The ground was prepared, and after the first mess I made of his dirt foundation, Mom really got after me and told me to stay off of it. The temptation was too great and I messed it up again.

This time Mom came after me with a little doubled-up cotton rope and I smarted off and told her she couldn't catch me. I took off for a big mesquite bush across the yard and crawled right up in the middle of it, thorns and all, and said, "Now you can't get me!" You know, that bush didn't seem to slow her down a bit, and I sure did get it. I can still remember it after well over 80 years. My first spanking (I only got two).

Daddy, with some jacks and some help, loaded that schoolhouse on some wagon wheels, hooked ten mules to it and headed across the road. Well, it was getting late in the evening and it got stuck in the sand and he said, "Okay, we will try again tomorrow." He had two more young mules he was just starting to break and said, "We will see what they are worth." So we came back with 12 mules. I was afraid it was going to break in the middle. Dad and I were sitting in the window and he drove the 12 mules looking down on them from above. I guess the young mules were pretty good because we got it moved. That old schoolhouse became our living room and the girls' bedroom.

A Cowboy Goes to War

2012 Photo of the schoolhouse.

Learning to back a trailer: While very young (preschool years) I had a tricycle and a little red wagon. The front end of the little wagon was damaged, so Dad took the front wheel assembly off and put a tongue on the front of the wagon and a hitch on the tricycle. The adults were talking about backing trailers, so my dad would lay kitchen chairs down as if they were a cattle-loading chute and I had to back my trailer in from all different angles. That training has really served me well. My rig is a lot bigger now, but I'm still backing after more than 80 years.

I started to school but couldn't see any reason for it at all. Why did I need to go to school to take care of those old cows? So I failed 2A and 2B—a full year, or two semesters in second grade.

In 1932 Franklin Delano Roosevelt (FDR) was running for President and it, was a big deal because Grandpa said, "Well, if that G.D.S.O.B. gets it I'll go to *Mexico*." I just knew I was going to lose my buddy. Well, FDR won, and it really made some changes in our lives, but Grandpa didn't go to *Mexico*.

Mamie's 4 girls and a boy. Ralph, Nadine, Muriel, Nettie, Alda

The *Taylor Grazing Act* went into effect, and we had to fence in the open range that had been allotted to us.

Under the new law, each rancher had to fence the land allotted to him and they told him how many cattle he was allowed to graze on it.

There was a lot of fence to build: cutting and hauling posts and wire in a wagon, digging post holes and in some cases blasting them. Of course I wasn't big enough to help much but I was there.

The Taylor Grazing Act really set in motion a rivalry between the ranchers. Each rancher was set up with land according to government guidelines they thought was fair to all, but of course each rancher didn't think he got his fair share.

So the war was on, and the courts were busy trying to keep peace on the range. In our case it was no different. There were hard feelings and court cases back and forth for a couple of generations but now the families are intermarried and working together. That first generation is gone and all seems to be okay.

During that time of turmoil, an incident happened that I remember so clearly it is like yesterday. I was about seven or eight years old, and my cousin Wayne Toney was down to visit from *Central*, and it was just after we had a good rain. Up on the main road above the ranch house we had a cattle guard with a big hole under it. Of course it was full of rainwater, and where there is rainwater there are frogs.

Being little boys we wanted some of those frogs. I was a skinny little kid, so I slipped down between the guard rails. My body would go through but my head wouldn't, so I caught some frogs with my toes and handed them up to Wayne.

We were having a good time until we saw a car coming and I was hanging there in the cattle guard with my head above the rails and my body below the rails and I couldn't go up or down. Wayne got out in the middle of the road and stopped the car. It was a rancher to the south, and he had been involved with us in land disputes. He was a very tall man and from my position he looked like a giant. I was scared to death because he was the enemy, and I thought this was the end of me.

He came over and got me by the shoulders and pulled me up out of the cattle guard and said, "I don't think this is a good place to play." He got in his new Buick and drove on down the road.

Wayne and I decided he wasn't so bad after all, but why did he buy a car instead of a pickup?

We forgot about the frogs.

~ ~ ~

The FDR administration set up a program to buy thousands of sheep from *Australia* and set ranchers up with sheep. The deal was that within two or three years you had to pay back a young sheep for each sheep you got. The sheep were shipped from *Australia* to the *West Coast* and driven across country.

At that time, Mom had about 200 head of very nice Rambouillet sheep. The sheep we were getting in the deal were Suffolk. Daddy had a little bunch of goats. I don't remember how many sheep we got, but altogether we had almost 1000 head of goats and sheep. The corrals were set up at the big gap. We had a lot of trouble with bobcats. When we found where they had killed a sheep, we didn't go close to it until Dad could set a trap by it. A cat would eat what it wanted and come back in two or three days for the rest. We caught several bobcats.

~ ~ ~

Hamp McDougal

On my 9th birthday, my Daddy said, "Ralph, if you are going to run this ranch someday it is time you start taking a more active part and learn what it is all about."

I think this is when my life really started. He woke me up.

He said, "Ralph, you and I are small, so we need to use our brain instead of our brawn, and with Christ's help we can do about anything."

About the last part of April, we had a good lamb crop and a good wool crop. On the 3rd, 4th, and 5th of May, we had a bad snowstorm and our sheep piled up in the corner of the corral and it killed most of them. For about three days we hauled dead sheep out into the canyon just north of the corrals with a 1928 Chevy coupe with a rumble seat.

There was no way Dad could continue with the sheep, so we took what he had left—Mom's 200 sheep, the new lambs, and sheep that survived the snow—up to the little gap at the north end of the mountain to wait for arrangements to be made for them to be picked up. We let them run free and checked on them often.

They made a deal on the sheep and the man hired me to take care of them until they could be shipped. I rode Brownie, a little brown mule, to herd them. Brownie and I did fine until he decided to throw me. I never learned to ride him, but he would always wait for me to get back on. I watched the sheep for eight days and the man gave me eight silver dollars. Man, was I rich! My dad said, "I guess we weren't meant to be in the sheep business."

A side benefit to the sheep being driven from a port on the *West Coast* across country is that they had filaree seed in their wool and it was spread clear across the southwest U.S. Filaree is a very good stock feed and it grows with very little water.

Wayne Toney, my cousin from *Central*, got to come down and spend some time with me. Wayne and I rode up to check on the sheep, and old Bob (a white collie) and one of Daddy's hounds went with us. On the way home, the dogs treed a bobcat in a big mesquite. So Wayne and I took our ropes and stretched him out and tied his mouth and feet up with baling wire. Then we tied him behind my saddle and took him home so Daddy could use him to train his dogs. When we got to the ranch, Aunt Ethel (Wayne's mom) was there and just had a fit. She got Wayne by the ear, marched him to the car and left. I didn't see Wayne again for some time. Two or three days later, we took the bobcat up to the flood tank, turned him loose and gave him about two hours head start. Daddy took his dogs up and put them on his trail. He got away. Never saw him again.

~ ~ ~

Think I should stop here and review a little. My memories before my 9th birthday are just incidents that I am not sure where they belong. I can't remember Mom being pregnant or giving birth. She had Eugene "stillborn" when I was 3, Luther when I was 6, and Dyar when I was 9.

I had some friends on the ranch: J.B. Hedrick, Calvin Cox, and Mary Ann Sebring. They were children of families Daddy took in. "Us boys" competed in peeing over a barbwire fence and Mary Ann got so upset because she couldn't do it. One time Calvin and I got into his mom's snuff bottle, and we ate it instead of dipping it. It made us oh-so-sick—maybe that is why I never liked tobacco…?

Dad leased some grassland called "The L.T." near where my nephew Cody lives now. My sister Nadine and I could play hide-and-seek in it because it was over our heads. In the fall, we would cut prairie hay and bale it. My job was to keep the mule going in circles to power the baler. There were little worms that crawled around in grass with lights on their tails like fireflies—glowworms.

One year after we were finished baling the hay, Daddy put some horses in The L.T. pasture for a while and one of them belonged to Mr. Watkins. When we tried to take them off the pasture, Mr. Watkins's horse would not go into the corral. So Dad got the family down to help corral him, but he kept running around us or between us. Daddy got his old sawed-off shotgun with double-ought buckshot in it and was going to use it to turn him. He ran off into the brush about 100 yards and we saw a big dust cloud. Yep, he was dead. It cost Daddy $25. As a comparison, Daddy bought the 1928 Chevrolet coupe for $25 and we drove it for years—the same one we hauled all the dead sheep out with, and the one I learned to drive in.

When we used to herd the goats and sheep down on Grandpa's place, we had a lot of trouble with them getting bit in the stomach by rattlesnakes because wild cowpeas grew up in the mesquite brush, and as the goats and sheep reared up on brush to eat the cowpeas the snakes would strike them in the belly. We would catch them and cut a little slit to make it bleed and hoped they would survive. They usually did. In 1932, we lost the sheep.

Daddy was a very smart man and a God-fearing man. I don't know how many schools he'd been to, but I do know he was a steam pipe fitter and sewing machine repairman.

This is mother and a big old sow with her cute little piglets.

Early in my life he had pigs. It was during prohibition because we went to trade boars with some people that lived just below *Bobcat Canyon*. When we got there, the pigs were acting very strange, and I asked Daddy what was wrong with them. I didn't think we wanted a pig like that. He said, "Keep quiet, I'll tell you later."

Well, they had a still. The water came from the Bottomless Swimming Hole up in *Bobcat Canyon*, and they were raising pigs on waste from the still, so the pigs were drunk. That is all I remember except Daddy lost his pigs to cholera. That was a big setback. Then he tried to get cattle started. The sheep deal came along so he went for that, and you know what happened to that.

So what was he to do? He had a wife, seven children, a mother-in-law, a father-in-law, and a father to take care of. Of course by this time due to FDR there was Social Security, and I can remember Granny's first check of $23. Boy, we thought she was rich!

Deer Hunting

Hunting was always a big thing in our lives. Daddy sure could tell some great hunting stories. He told them so well that we couldn't remember for sure if we were there or not.

Daddy was always a good shot and fast with his little 25-20. Of course at target shooting, Mom could outshoot him. Daddy took the back sight off his 25-20. He said it was just in the way. He had other guns, but the 25-20 was his deer hunting rifle. It would hold a lot of ammo. If he had the magazine full, that was all he needed for a season. He very seldom fired more than one shot to get a deer. He could see and shoot a deer before the rest of us really knew what was going on. Almost like a quick draw.

One of Daddy's stories I remember was when he was a guide. He would take a person hunting and pack them into the *Gila Wilderness*, guarantee them a shot at a deer, take care of their deer and pack them out for $25. This was the middle 1920s or early 1930s.

He said they had several horses and mules to get from the ranch to the *Gila* so he had Alda and a couple of ranch hands drive them almost 100 miles. They stopped overnight at the McSherry apple orchards up on the *Mimbres River*. The people would have their own bedrolls and tents and hunting gear but he would limit it. Daddy did the supplying of the food and did the cooking. It would be an early breakfast, a packed lunch, and a big campfire supper. If someone got a deer it was a tradition to have fried liver and heart, Dutch oven bisquits and gravy and some kind of canned vegetable. On the way packing in, Daddy would kill a deer for camp meat, so they ate a lot of venison. You must remember, Daddy had a lot of help from Alda and a couple of hands and there wouldn't be more than 3 or 4 clients, but some of them were stinkers.

Daddy would have all of the livestock in the corral and well fed the night before and ready to hit the road at daylight in the morning. They drove them along beside the roads, which were before pavement and very little traffic. It would take a good 3 days to get from the ranch to set up in the *Black Range*. Oh yes, there were some fences, but they all had gates, remember the horse was as much in use as was the motor vehicle, at that time.

I guess about the second night in camp there was some real excitement. He had a little gray mare that sorta kept the horses and mules together, so he could hobble the mare and turn the others loose and they would stay close. After supper with the stock all settled in for the night and a fire going with everyone sitting around—I am sure telling stories—it happened. A panther squealed, and of course horses and mules are scared to death of panthers. The horses and mules stampeded and came right through the camp over fire, tents, and all. As they came through the camp, Daddy grabbed "Old Buck," his favorite mule, around the neck and hung on until Alda could get a rope around Old Buck's neck. The rest of the stock was still running with the little gray mare leaping with her hobbles. They got their camp back in some kind of order and at daylight Daddy got on Old Buck and followed the trail of the missing stock. He found them about 3 or 4 miles down the way headed for home.

I am not sure if it was the same hunt that they lost Joe Norton. Joe Norton was the fiancé of a school teacher in *Deming* and had come west for his health. Daddy set Joe up with "Dunny," a small dun mule, very gentle but a real character. Daddy gave Joe one spur of a pair and told him to be sure and not lose it because he had given its mate to someone else. Daddy said, "If you get off to walk, take the spur off and hang it on the saddle."

Joe wasn't feeling very good and just wanted to make a short hunt. Daddy suggested an area for him to hunt and sent him off with water and a lunch. Well, everyone went their way hunting and ended up back in camp along toward evening, and here came Dunny into camp without Joe. The spur was hung on the saddle, but the water and lunch wasn't there. Needless to say they spread out and hunted for Joe, firing a gun in the air every so often, but never got an answer. They hunted for Joe for about 2 weeks, and finally gave up. A few days later, the school teacher got a group together to go back in. Daddy furnished horses and they hired Alda as a guide. I think they hunted about another 2 weeks without success. Almost 20 years later, some hunters found his rifle and bones in some very thick brush in the area.

So what did really happen? Did Dunny run off and leave him? If so, where was the water and lunch? The spur was on the saddle, so he must have been off walking. If Joe was just sick, why didn't he answer the shots? Had he got a deer or a bear and was hurt by a wounded animal? Did he commit suicide? Did he have a heart attack? I guess we will never know what really happened. This happened about 80 years ago so I don't know of anyone but Nadine and I that will remember.

Think I need to tell what and how hobbles are used. Hobbles are sorta like a large pair of handcuffs. They are put on the front feet of a horse or mule limiting them to only short steps, so won't travel very far. But when they panic, they start leaping or lunging similar to the way a dog or a rabbit runs.

I don't think Daddy did much guide work after the Joe Norton incident.

One year before I was old enough to hunt, Daddy took me with him and Mr. Tanner to hunt up on the *North Star Mesa* in the *Gila National Forest*. Mr. Tanner was a traveling salesman that had a big car—a Durant. It had a 4-speed transmission and was a big boxy car with 4 doors, a gas tank that stuck out behind with a trunk on top of it. He also had a trailer made out of a very similar car. He had taken the engine and front wheels off it and put a tongue on it so he had a good enclosed trailer. Mr. Tanner would buy citrus fruit and honey in *California* and head east, selling it till he ran out, then he would go back for another load. Well, Mr. Tanner was at the ranch when deer season came around, and he wanted to go hunting. So he and Daddy took the trunk off the back of that big old Durant and made a little stock rack back there. They put a donkey in the stock rack, and the three of us headed for the *North Star Mesa*.

Just before getting to the *North Star Mesa* there's a pretty steep hill to climb, and Mr. Tanner had that Durant down in granny gear. We were slow and noisy, but we were really climbing that hill. Well, here came Uncle Jim up behind us in a new Ford V-8, really coming on fast. And of course he couldn't pass us, so he came on up and started pushing us. Mr. Tanner says, "That is okay, let him push. We don't need his help but let him think he is helping, it will save us some gas and we will both be happy."

A Cowboy Goes to War

At that time for a $5.00 hunting license you could get one deer, one bear, two turkeys, and five squirrels. I remember we came out with some game, but I don't remember just what. By the time we got ready to come out, it had rained and snowed until the roads were very bad, so we waited until about 2:00 in the morning when everything would be frozen. We made it fine.

One year when Luther was just a toddler and Grandpa was about 79 years old, we had one fine deer hunt. Daddy built a trailer that could carry 3 donkeys and be pulled by a Model A Ford. We— Daddy, Mom, Grandpa, Luther, me, Nadine, Muriel and Charles Hamilton (nicknamed "Grasshopper")—headed for the *Gila*. We camped the first night on *Mimbres River* just below where Luther's house is now. We got up the next morning ready to take on the *North Star Mesa* hill. Everyone got out to walk up the hill so the Model A could pull the hill—except Daddy, Mom, and Luther. Of course the donkeys had to walk too. In fact one of them had to carry Grandpa.

Next morning we loaded the donkeys and hit the *Reeds Peak* trail. About the middle of the afternoon we made camp and Daddy took a walk to check for deer signs. He was gone a long time, in fact he didn't get back till nearly dark. His report was not very good. He said our best chance to get a deer was to go Indian hunting. That meant putting extra blankets under the donkeys' pack saddles, take a frying pan, salt and pepper and a little flour for making gravy and live off the land.

We set out pretty early the next morning. Daddy was in the lead with Grandpa riding a donkey and the rest of us following with the other 2 donkeys (Mom and Luther stayed in camp). Daddy was very good with that 25-20 rifle. He said the back sight got in his way so he took it off and only used the front sight. He very seldom had to use a second shot. He would shoot so quick that you almost didn't see him. When he was guiding, he would show a hunter a deer and the hunter would get buck fever and start shooting; Daddy would snap shoot and holler, "You got him! You got him!"—the hunter would never know the difference. Along toward evening Daddy pulled his snap shooting and got a little whitetail deer. About a 4 point. We hunted both the big mule deer that have big ears, a small tail and forked antlers, and the whitetailed sometimes called a fan-tailed, ears are a bit smaller, a large white tail, branched antlers, and as a rule a smaller deer.

So we ate after all. We had heart, liver, and gravy for supper and again for breakfast. For lunch we had venison steaks and gravy. We were very comfortable with this diet. We got a lot of exercise and it contained a lot of fat, so we had no trouble.

The nights got well below freezing, so we set up against a log on a hillside with a fire just below us. One person stayed awake to keep the fire going while the others tried to sleep. We all took turns at the fire. You never did get much sleep because you would be hot on one side and cold on the other, so you would keep turning. Oh yes, we had some blankets but not nearly enough. Oh the nights were so pretty! The stars were so big and bright, and we were so high we felt like we were looking down on the rest of the world.

The second evening we ran into a fence camp. Two men had a pretty nice camp set up. They were fence builders. That night and the next morning we sure did eat. We had Dutch oven biscuits, honey, and syrup to go with our venison steaks and gravy. Nadine was eating with a spoon and she wanted to get some honey. She looked at the spoon, then at the honey, and one of the fence builders winked at her and said, "Just lick it off and go ahead!" She did and Muriel just about had a fit. I don't think Nadine ever lived that down. That hunt has always been a very fond memory, even though we got so little game.

Two or three years later we had a very similar setup. The Model A, the trailer, three donkeys, Daddy, Mom, Luther, (Dyar?) me, Nadine, and someone else. Daddy said we were going to drive "until we find game." We were way up in the *Gila* with me and someone else riding on the back of the trailer, ready to get off and push if necessary. When we started off into *Rocky Canyon*, the hill was pretty steep and that old Model A didn't have very good brakes. What a ride we had down that curvy dirt road! We were plenty scared when we got to the bottom. About the time we got stopped, someone hollered "Deer!" and pointed up the hill. Sure nuff, two 4-point mule deer. The scramble for guns started. We really don't know who got what, but Daddy shot twice, so if nobody else hit them, he did. One of them had been shot 11 times with 22 shorts. The slugs were just under the skin but he had healed up okay.

We got off the road and made camp. The next morning I walked out on a small bluff and almost straight down below me were several deer in an oak grove, feeding. Among them was a nice 6-point mule deer. I shot almost straight down on him in the right shoulder and was sure he was mine so I didn't shoot again, I didn't want to spoil any more meat. Well, he took off running through the brush with his right front leg flopping. I trailed him all day and part of the next morning, but I never did get him. We had plenty of game but I hated to leave him to suffer.

One year when I was in my middle teens, Daddy said we couldn't go hunting that year, but some of our neighbors wanted to borrow some horses to go hunting. Daddy said, "Only if you take Ralph with you to take care of the horses." There was a boy about my age, Ralph Graff, and we did fine together. We got in late in the evening, so I was up before daylight to find water for the horses. I dropped off into the canyon below camp and started my way up to find water and I noticed something wasn't quite right. I could outline several turkeys in the trees. So I shot one and he came flopping down then the big flock flew down and headed up the hill to the north, so I took after them on foot. Right up that steep hill. Well, just before I got to the top of the hill I finally got a shot and got me another turkey. I carried my prize to the top of the ridge and watched the flock soar off down into the canyon. What a beautiful sight!

Ralph McDougal

I was so tired my tongue was hanging out and I was breathing very heavy, but I stopped to clean my turkey and looked up—there stood 5 deer, three bucks and 2 does. I picked out one and shot but I completely missed and I now had only one cartridge left so I really took care and shot again. The deer dropped in his tracks, so with my turkey in hand, I took off to claim my deer—but before I got to him he started trying to get up. I dropped my turkey, laid my gun down and pulled my knife. I wasn't about to let him get away. When I got to him he was struggling to get up. I got his antler in my left hand and reached over with my right and cut his throat. But he got me with his hind foot and peeled my right arm from my elbow to my knuckle. That's okay, I had my deer and 2 turkeys and the season wasn't 2 hours old. After dressing the turkey and deer I had to go back and find my other turkey and get the horses to pack out the deer. It didn't work that way. I spent hours looking for that turkey and never did find it.

We spent several days and I assisted them in getting two more bucks and another turkey, but then Ralph and I had to get back to school. Ralph and I took 2 deer, 2 turkeys, and 2 horses and went home. The rest of the group stayed to hunt. A few days later when they came out they had a buck to show, but they tried to sneak out 3 does. They got caught and fined pretty heavy. I never saw them again.

About the time Daddy started to work in *El Paso* our deer hunting became more local. One year we had a small group of deer that hung out in the little canyon where the chip tank is. There were two little 4-point bucks in the group. With some planning, we were up in that canyon about sunup. Very shortly we jumped the deer and the shooting started. One buck went down pretty quick, but the other one was just wounded but left a good trail to the south. We found him hid in some brush near where the red tank is now. I was going to shoot him and Daddy yelled, "Wait a minute!" He sat Luther up on a big rock so he could see the deer in the brush and gave him a 30-30. He says, "This is Luther's deer." It seemed like it took Luther forever to shoot, and when he did, the 30-30 kicked so hard it almost knocked Luther off that rock backwards. Oh yes, he got the deer all right.

Along about this time, while riding between the ranch and the big gap, Nadine and I kept seeing this little group of deer that had the most beautiful big buck leading it that we named him The Rocking Chair Buck. His rack did resemble a rocking chair. But when deer season came we couldn't find him. However, he survived that season and we got to watch him another year. We couldn't find him the next season either. Someone must have gotten him because we didn't see him again.

Water Witching

Mamie water witching (dowsing) in 1960.

We never had a very good well on the ranch and the folks decided to get it witched (water witching or dowsing), to find underground water with a forked stick. They got Doc Smyer to come over and spot a well for us. Well, Doc started going over the place and Mom asked him if she could try it. That is the way it started.

Doc and Mom worked for a little while and Doc took his sticks and went home. He told Daddy that Mom was better at it than he was.

She just needed some practice. Boy, she got it! She dowsed all over the country. That is when she witched the well in Dyar's north field.

When they put the pump in that well to test pump it, Daddy was out there with his shovel trying to save the water. Mom was really good at it. They got enough for ranch and home use but not enough for big farming.

My first well was in 1950 in *Anapra* near *El Paso*. It was in an area of many dry wells and mine turned out good. So my witching career had its start.

Water witching is very good, but it is not perfect. We estimate that I have witched about 350 wells, but we have had two dry wells. And of course one of them had to be Denny and Karla's (my nephew and his wife) in Oregon. The other one was Irven Valdez, east of *Tularosa* near the Indian Reservation. Both had similar terrain, "volcanic". While witching for a well on the ranches, we might walk miles before finding a location that was satisfactory for a well.

Chapter 2
Works Progress Administration

By this time Dad was really getting desperate and FDR had come out with the *Works Progress Administration* (WPA). A project was in the mill to build a water control dam, *Bassett Lake*, just below what is now my nephew Monty's farm. Dad applied to furnish three 4-mule teams and tools. The mule skinners were any able-bodied man with a family, but Daddy could only work a man three days a week and another man got to work the other three days—that way each man got a little bit of work.

Daddy went down and set up a tent and built corrals. When school was out, I joined him and he called me his wrangler. My job was to feed and water the 12 mules and to look them over good to make sure they were okay. We worked nine hours a day, six days a week, with an hour for lunch. That hour included unhitching the mules which I watered and fed a quart of oats. Then they would hitch them up and work another four hours.

The goat that went with us on the job had a dual purpose. Her job was to ward off diseases (sickness) for our mules and to furnish Daddy and me milk for the camp. I don't know whether they still do it or not, but people liked to keep a goat with their fine horses. They believed that since goats were almost never sick that they would keep their horses from getting sick. The goat would stay with the mules except when we went home on Sunday. The goat would ride on the front of the car between the fender and the engine hood and tied to the light. She would stand leaning against the hood with her feet braced against the fender. As for riding on the fender, the cars were made different then. She seemed to like it. I didn't see anybody else doing that.

WPA didn't work Sundays. We had a tent right down by the corrals.

My dad was the cook for the two of us—we would build a fire with mesquite wood, cook lots of beans and boiled potatoes and usually had some kind of meat. Mesquite wood holds its heat for a long time and we cooked the beans for a long time. We started cooking them and by the end of the week, they were soup. Daddy was a terrific cook in the Dutch oven. We had lots of biscuits and gravy, and we'd have bacon gravy ... he used bacon mostly for seasoning. The gravy was made with goat's milk. Oh boy did it taste good!

~ ~ ~

During that summer we had some **real** sandstorms and thunderstorms. I learned to drive that old 1928 Chevy and how to swim. That Chevy had three speeds on the floor, and it would pop out of gear on rough roads, so Daddy fixed a stick to go between the dash and stick shift to keep it in gear.

After the first good thunderstorm, we had a good-sized body of water behind the dam. It was about nine feet deep near the dam, but it got shallow not far out from the dam and covered several acres.

I had about three hours of spare time in the morning and afternoon after taking care of the mules, so I spent it playing in the lake. I learned to swim, and with two crossties left over from building the corrals, I made a raft fastened together with 2 x 4's and a GI feedbox for a seat. I could use a long-handled shovel as a paddle and go all over that lake. One of the mule skinners brought his dog along and he liked to go with me on the raft. Oh, it was fun!

When summer was over I had to go back to school, but I went back with a different look on life as if I had woken up. I started taking part in school and my grades greatly improved. The dam wasn't finished, so I went to school by driving the '28 Chevy every day for a few days. Daddy made arrangements with Mrs. Bell from the little store across the street from the school so I could park there and still go to school.

The next summer, Dad made arrangements for FDR's CCC (Civilian Conservation Corp) boys to build stock trails up to the top of the mountain. I only remember two of them, the *West Trail* and the *South* or *Big Gap Trail*. The *West Trail* started just south of where Nadine's house is now and came out on top just north of the peak with all the towers. It was pretty steep, but it was a good trail. At one point it goes through a rock slide and they were afraid the CCC boys would get hurt, so Daddy, Luther and I had to build the trail across the rock slide while they watched us. Luther was getting to be a big help.

Ralph McDougal

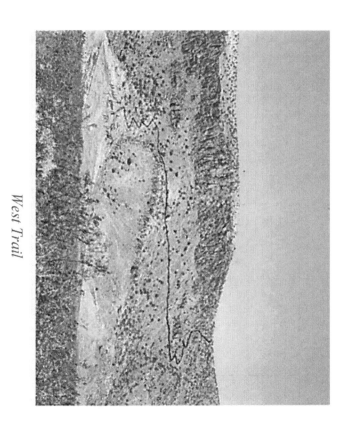

West Trail

A Cowboy Goes to War

That Christmas Daddy was working someplace and wasn't available so Nadine, Luther and I took a little red wagon and went up just above where Nadine's house is now and got a Christmas tree. It seemed a lot farther back pulling that Christmas tree than it did going up. I don't know why we didn't have horses.

When I was 10 years old, Daddy said, "Ralph, it is time to learn to be a cowboy, so you break horses as you ride the ranch." Well, Kretiks had a little gray mare that they had spoiled rotten and when they tried to ride her she threw them off. So Daddy said, "We'll break her for you."

When Dad had a real bad or wild horse, it took two or three people to hold it to put a saddle on. He'd have a rope on it but it would really fight having a saddle put on it. So he would "ear it down". Sometimes all the way down but usually only until they got the saddle on. I started on the right side of the horse and then put my left arm over the horse's neck and held its left ear in my left hand. I would then hold its right ear in my teeth and get its nose in my right hand. Yes, I didn't touch the ground much, I just hung on! This controls or distracts the bronc long enough for the cowboy to get the saddle on him and to get in the saddle. Then they turn it loose.

The little gray mare didn't need all of this, but Daddy was making me feel like a cowboy. When I say she just goaded out there with me, I am saying she didn't try very hard to throw me, she just jumped a little. Daddy and some guy eared her down and made a big show of saddling her. They put me on her, opened the gate and turned her loose. Well, she goaded out there a little ways and she and I got to be good friends ... I really thought I was a cowboy. Many horses later, I knew better.

Chapter 3
Hamp's First Team

My dad would often tell me about his first team. It doesn't seem like much now, but he sure was proud of it—a horse and a donkey in sort of a mismatch. He would load his buckboard with fruits and vegetables grown in the *Mesilla Valley* by *Las Cruces, New Mexico*, and take them up to *Silver City, New Mexico*, about 120 miles to the west/northwest where he would peddle them to the miners. It would take him a week or more to make a round trip. He was 19 years old then and just getting started.

Just before *Hurley, New Mexico*, the highway curves toward the north across a dry streambed. Daddy said that stream used to have water in it up to the belly of his team. Wait a minute, he had a donkey and a horse. Which belly was he talking about?

A Cowboy Goes to War

Ralph McDougal

On his way back from *Silver City,* at the little village of *"Old Town"* (now a ghost town), Dad saw my mother for the first time.

My mom and dad dressed up to go someplace special.

She was the most beautiful 16-year-old blond girl he had ever seen. She was walking home from school and he tried to get close enough to talk to her, but she crawled through a barbed wire fence and ran off.

A while later they were having a dance at *Old Town* and Daddy made a point to be there. That is where they got together. He never told me about their romance, but it must have been pretty good because it lasted till Mom died at the age of 72.

*Love
that
lasted a
lifetime.*

My mom could ride and shoot.

Mom was One Wonderful Woman

I don't think there was anything my mom couldn't do.

In the late 1920s when things were tight, a circus came to *Deming* and set up just east of town by the railroad. Of course "us kids" asked to go. Daddy said, "We don't have time for that kind of foolishness. We have work to do."

But Mom said, "We are going." So we kids and Mom piled into that old Model T with Dad yelling, "Be careful of those brakes!"… and we were off.

That circus had the biggest tent you can imagine, with the animals out back. They had wooden panel walls with a canvas top, and posts laying on the ground up near the wooden panels to form a parking area. When we got there, there was only one parking spot left. Mom rushed in to get it, but when she put on the brakes, there were none, so the front end jumped the parking post and right through one of the wooden panels and there we sat—our front wheels in the animal pen and the back wheels were where the front wheels should have been. By the way, the circus was great. We just sat bug-eyed.

Along about that same time, Mom and some of "us kids" were in the Model T going up to see Granny at *Ft. Bayard*. We got as far as *Faywood Hot Springs* and had car trouble. We spent the night at the Faywood Hotel.

~   ~   ~

Mom was a real good vet. We had a long-horned milk cow and just after I fed her, a ewe from the next pen got in with her and she proceeded to rip that sheep wide open. Her guts were dragging on the ground. I yelled for Mom. By the time she got there I was holding the sheep. Mom looked the sheep over and said, "Just hold her and I'll be right back." Very shortly she was back with a pan of Lysol water, an upholstery needle and thread. We cleaned the sheep guts up real good and stuffed them back in her and Mom sewed her up while I held her. In just a few days she was back to normal.

Mom's hair was long and blond, clear down past her waist. She wrapped it up in a big bun at the back of her head. The girls, my sisters, talked her into cutting it off, and she never grew it long again. Maybe it was easier to keep, but I liked it long.

She was always very concerned when "us kids" would be out on the ranch. We would leave the ranch house by sunup with a job to get done, such as check water and account for all the stock, and check to see that they were all right. If they were hurt or sick, we would take care of them if possible. Sometimes we had to go back the next day with what was needed to take care of them. We had to make sure they had plenty of water and salt (which made the stock fatten better), and make sure they were not overgrazing a certain area.

At times we would run into some kind of problem and wouldn't be finished before nightfall, so we had a system for letting Mom know. We would go to the top of the *West Trail* and if we were going to spend the night, we would light just one fire. If we were coming in, we would light a second fire a ways down the trail. Mom would know that we were coming in, and she would have time to have a good supper waiting for us. To get down the mountain from the top of *West Trail* would take about an hour or a little more. Getting off the mountain was slow, particularly after dark. We couldn't see at all so the horses had to pick the way. But boy, when the horses hit the flats, they really would take off—dark or not!—and we let them have their head and hung on. The horses knew that they had grain, hay, water, and no saddle waiting for them, so they were in a hurry. The signal for emergency was three fires. We thank the Lord that we never had to use that. The Lord was with us and we were always able to take care of things.

~ ~ ~

The "three fires" was used only one time. Daddy was up at the goat camp by himself and the eagles were after the kid goats, so Daddy decided to destroy their nests. The nests were up in the bluffs and he couldn't get to them from below or above, so he got on top of the bluff and lit a Sotol cactus and dropped it down into the eagles' nest. It set the eagles' nest on fire and part of it fell out of the nest and was burning at the bottom of the bluff. So he had three fires— one on top of the bluff, one in the eagles' nest, and one at the bottom of the bluff. Those three fires were on the east side of the mountain and couldn't be seen from the ranch, but our friends, the Sincombs, lived on the east side of the mountain and they saw the three fires. They came hauling over to the ranch to see what was going on, and of course by this time it was well after dark. Several men got together and headed for the goat camp which was about a 2 ½ or 3-hour climb in the dark. Daddy was asleep in his bedroll when they woke him up. He was shocked to see them, because he had no idea what he had done—he couldn't see the bottom of the bluff. All was well but it was a busy night.

Fires were very simple to light, even in any kind of weather. The dry leaves on the Sotol cactus plant are high in alcohol content and grow in such a way that up under the dead leaves it will always be dry and ready to start a fire. The Sotol is very plentiful all over the *Little Florida Mountains*.

Alda and the Pinch Bar

Once my family was all in the car and we were going someplace special. At that time the road went from the ranch house north to a water control dam that Daddy had at the end of the field. After we went over the dam the road made a sharp right to the east.

After passing over the dam, Daddy tried to turn right, there was a snap and we just kept going north out into the mesquite brush until Daddy could get the car stopped. After looking things over and getting out of the sand, Daddy put Alda up on the left front fender with a pinch bar (sometimes called a crowbar) and she would steer the car by tapping the front or back side of the front wheel with the pinch bar while Daddy drove the car. We got back to the house okay, but "us kids" missed an outing.

A pinch bar was a very handy thing on the ranch.

Fun Time After Supper

When things were slow or for some reason we had time after supper, we would sit in the living room by a big wood heater and by coal-oil lamp and read aloud or tell stories. Daddy was an outstanding storyteller and of course he was the hero when he was telling the story. Maybe this is where Luther gets his storytelling talent.

Sometimes the girls (mostly Alda and Nettie) would read, while the entire family sat spellbound. We heard a lot of the Zane Grey books. At times there were other storytellers, but none of them was as good as Daddy. These sessions only happened if for some reason we couldn't work at doing something else.

~ ~ ~

One of Daddy's stories was Pancho Villa's Raid. In 1916, Pancho Villa raided *Columbus, New Mexico*. At the time Daddy was in the National Guard in *Deming*, about 32 miles north of *Columbus*. The National Guard rushed down by auto and horses and mules to push Pancho Villa and his men back into *Mexico*.

When Daddy got there, Pancho Villa and his men were ready to run, but the Guard only followed a short ways into *Mexico*. Daddy said a short way below *Columbus* a young Mexican, that had been holding the horses for Pancho and his officers, lay wounded. Daddy pulled him up under a bush and gave him some water and emergency rations then proceeded on with his unit.

When the unit got back to *Columbus*, they had the job of cleaning up after the battle. Daddy said not many U.S. citizens were killed, but quite a few of the Mexicans were killed. The railroad went through *Columbus* so they had a lot of crossties available. The bodies of the dead and badly wounded Mexicans were thrown on the crossties and burned. This really bothered Daddy. When things quieted down a little, Daddy went back over and got the young Mexican he had left under the bush and brought him back to *Deming*.

Ralph McDougal

By the time I knew the young Mexican, he was living *in Silver City* and to me he was an old man. What I remember most was his very heavy eyelids. He kept them propped open with little sticks.

Chapter 4
The Hay Baler

The hay baler at that time was mule-powered with one mule going around and around in a circle, keeping the rod arm moving back and forth. We could adjust the piston stroke by moving the rod bearing in or out on the rod arm. The guide line kept the mule going in a circle and the piston rod was in a box or housing and was covered with dirt so the mule had to go over a small hump. We adjusted the draw arm so the mule was going down when he had the hardest pull. My job was to keep the mule going, but he would always stop on the other side of the circle. I would have to run around to keep him moving … so I ended up riding the mule.

The piston stroke was just about as long as the hopper opening, so the piston would go pretty slow. One person would feed the hopper and set the wire feed blocks which would determine the size of bales.

This meant one person would be on each side of the compression cylinder. As I remember it, the man on the right side had a big roll of baling wire and a long ¼ inch steel rod. He would pass the wire through the wire feed slot to the person on the other side who would send it back on the other side of the bale. The first man would tie it and then cut it. This had to be done for a top and bottom wire of each bale. We would end up with a very neat bale of hay and as heavy as the hopper feeder wanted. "Us kids" always wanted a small person on the hopper so he wouldn't make the bales so heavy. We had to keep the bales clear from the end of the baler.

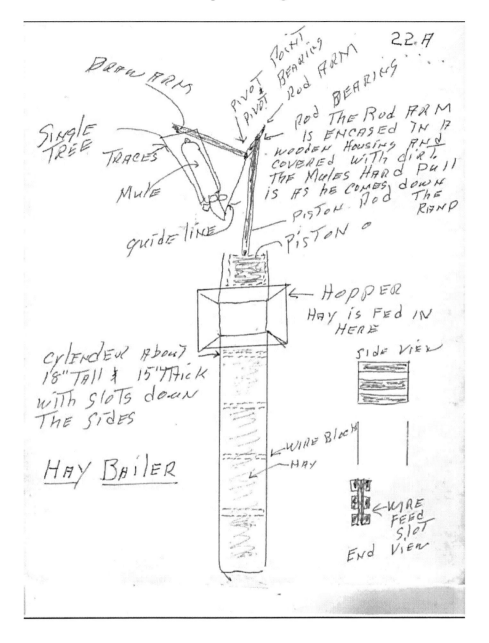

DRAW ARM

PIVOT POINT
PIVOT BEARING
Rod ARM

22.A

SINGLE TREE

TRACES

Mule

Rod BEARING

Rod THE Rod ARM
IS ENCASED IN A
WOODEN HOUSING AND
COVERED WITH dirt.
THE MULES HARD PULL
IS AS he COMES down
THE RAMP

guide line

PISTON Rod

PISTON o

HOPPER

HAY is FED IN HERE

CYLENDER About
18" TALL & 15" THICK
with SLOTs down
THE SIDES

SIDE VIEW

HAY BAILER

WIRE BLOCK

HAY

WIRE FEED SLOT

End VIEW

Chapter 5
FDR-ism

Another FDR-ism came about from the high rabbit population. Of course that caused a high coyote population. Well FDR put a bounty on coyotes and rabbits. I think it was four cents each on rabbit and four dollars on coyotes. We had to produce both ears still attached together for payment.

Several things came from this. Daddy set up a wire fence trap in the northwest corner of the field. When the McDougals from all over the country came to visit, we had a rabbit drive and we sure caught a lot of rabbits. Then Nadine and I started trapping. The coyotes and the great horned owls were stealing the rabbits out of our traps. Well we would set another trap just out of the path of the rabbit and when the coyote came to eat our rabbit we would sometimes catch him. Daddy suggested that to catch the horned owls we could get a long 2 x 4 and tie it to a fence post to get it up high, and set a trap on top of it. "The owl will land on the highest point and get caught."

We didn't want to hurt the owl, so he said, "Okay, wrap cloth around the jaws of the trap and use a small #2 trap. Fasten the end of the trap chain near the top of the 2 x 4. Don't fasten the trap tight to the top of the 2 x 4. When the owl gets caught, he will try to fly off with the trap but can't, so you will find him hanging unharmed." The first one we caught was a big male and we wanted to keep him. So we made a cage to put him in. A few days later we caught a female and decided that was Mrs. Owl and put them in together. "Well she is his Mrs. Owl now."

It was a big job feeding them, so when somebody from town spread the word around, we sold them to one of the bars in town for $2.00 each. We got a request for two more and it took us awhile but we finally got them and got $2.00 each for them too. We had to run our trapline before school because Daddy said it would be cruel to leave an animal suffering all day.

We had a couple of little single shot .22 rifles. Daddy would give us three cartridges and give us three more for each rabbit we killed. If they were cottontails and we shot them in the head we would eat them, but if they were jack rabbits or not shot in the head we would feed them to the dogs or pigs or fish. Our earth tank had catfish in it and after we took the rabbits ears off, we would tie a wire to their hind leg, pull their skin off, and hang them in the tank with the catfish. In about an hour we could go back and pull the skeleton out of the water.

~ ~ ~

Daddy had two good bloodhounds, Queeny and Sport, and from them he got a nice litter of five. They got out on the road and one of them got hit, so he couldn't sell him. Jewel Butler, a rancher south of us, didn't want him. We named him Drum, and he was a real pet and got all kinds of special treatment and grew bigger than the other dogs.

Nadine and I ran our trapline one Wednesday morning, and a coyote had gotten away with one of our traps. We had to go to school so we couldn't go after him till Saturday. We put a dog chain on old Drum. We could still pick up the drag mark of the coyote with our trap, and it wasn't long till Drum picked up the scent and took off. Nadine, Luther, our youngest brother Dyar and I had the chain. First we lost Dyar and Nadine let go to take care of Dyar, and then Luther fell down and let go and I didn't last much longer.

A Cowboy Goes to War

By the time we got to him, Drum was standing there with the coyote in his mouth with the trap hanging down waiting for us. After a show or two like this, Jewel Butler came back and Daddy sold our great pet to him for $40, which was big money back then. I understand he made a very good bear dog. We caught several coyotes and sold a bunch of rabbit ears.

Chapter 6
Native Vegetation on the Ranch

Dad with wagonload of Sotol.

Sotol:

Ailing stock do well on Sotol and it is a quick, easy fire source. In the spring of the year after a long dry winter, the first green thing to come up was mustard weed. If the cattle ate too much of this fresh green mustard, they would go temporarily blind. Daddy would pen them up and feed them prairie hay along with Sotol cactus and cottonseed meal. The Sotol cactus is very much like Yucca.

Daddy would chop the head off the cactus and we could pull each leaf off the head. It was a long stickery leaf with a very edible spoon on the inside end of it about the size of our hand. It was Nadine's and my job to peel off a leaf, fill it with cottonseed meal and put it to the nose of the blind animal. They seemed to like it very well, and in a week or a little less they could see well enough to put them back on the mountain with the rest of the cattle.

I don't think we ever had more than about five blind cattle at a time, and the mustard was soon replaced by better range feed.

Yucca:

The roots of the Yucca were a fine source for making a hair soap. I dug many a root for my four sisters. Chop the root up a bit, put it in water, bring it to a boil and thin it to the consistency desired. It will make hair soft and shiny. In the spring the blooms go very good in salads. Bumble bees would make their nest in a Yucca pole by making a hole in the side and cleaning out space enough in the pole for their nest. As kids we would watch a bumble bee go into its hole and we would stuff a rock into the hole. Then we would break the pole off the Yucca plant. We now had a musical walking stick. That old bee would sure sing!

Prickly Pear:

In dry times, we used a Prickly Pear burner to burn off the thorns to make cattle feed (the farmers still use it to kill weeds, but they call it a weed burner). It burned white gas similar to the way Coleman stoves used to work. A tank hung on our shoulder with about a four-foot small pipe with a burner on the end of it. We pressured up the tank and lit the burner, and when it got to going right it made a lot of noise. Boy every cow in hearing distance would come running! They sure knew what to do with that warm de-thorned Prickly Pear. The goats, sheep, and deer would eat the Prickly Pear—thorns and all. But the cattle wouldn't eat it like that very much.

We would take the Model T up as close to the Prickly Pear as we could get, use the burner to burn the thorns off, cut off as many

"Mickey Mouse" leaves as we could carry on a pitchfork and take them to the Model T. We would get several hundred pounds at a time and they were pretty heavy. We used it for the milk cow. Prickly Pear is very juicy and it will sure make that cow give more milk. To prepare it for the cow, we would take a leaf about the size of a dinner plate in our left gloved hand, and with a machete in our right, we cut that leaf into about one-inch strips. Oh yes, we did cut a few fingers—my left forefinger has never been the same. We then put cottonseed meal on the cactus strips. We prepared a full five-gallon can morning and night.

The Prickly Pear apples (tunas) were delicious to eat and make jelly, syrup, and wine. To care for a bad sunburn, take a leaf that has been burned off, split it open to make two pads, and rub it on the sunburn generously. It will do every bit as good as aloe vera.

The game department introduced the ibex (Iranian goat) into the *Florida Mountains* several years ago, and they are really thinning out the Prickly Pear. People are now hard-pressed to find a ripe Prickly Pear apple.

Cow Peas and Pie Melons:

Years ago we had Cow Peas that grew up in the mesquite bushes and were a very good goat and sheep feed. We also had what they called a Pie Melon, shaped like a round ball about six to eight inches in diameter, light green with darker green stripes. It was sort of like a watermelon that never got ripe. It didn't have much taste to it and it wasn't juicy like a watermelon, but the goats and sheep sure did like them.

Parsley (Purslane) and Milkweed:

The goats and sheep liked both of these. What we called Parsley was a round, flat leaf about the size of a quarter. It grew from a center root with five or six stems close to the ground, about five or six inches long. Each stem would have several leaves on it in different stages of maturity. The stems were light green, and the leaves started out light, getting darker as they matured and became dark green. Milkweed was a very small, thick plant with little white flowers, less than an inch high, with many runners about five or six inches long. It was almost solid and about the size of a dinner plate. The plant stuck together pretty good. A goat could lift up one side of the plant and keep chewing until it had eaten the entire plant. It had a milky sap.

Greasewood (Chaparral):

Greasewood grows over most of the drier southwest *United States* and north central *Mexico*. As the grassland recedes, the Greasewood takes over. It is not a stock feed. They will not eat it. We use it as a tea to control "arthritis" – dried leaves and small stems. Put a good teaspoonful in a couple cups of water, bring to a boil, let cool, strain into a quart jar and finish filling the jar with water. We use 5 oz. morning and night for several days until we quit hurting, and we may not have to take it again for four or five months. "Oh my goodness it is nasty, but if we hurt bad enough we would drink it it. Reference: Medicinal Plants by Michael Moore.

Ephedra (Mormon tea, Cowboy tea, Squaw tea, Indian tea, Navaho tea):

Take your pick, it is all the same. It is a pleasant-tasting tea and is extremely good for the urinary system. The plant is very tough, almost impossible to cut with a knife. Daddy had a big gallon coffee pot. Since it was hard to cut up, he would wad up a pretty good handful of it and stuff it in that pot and fill the pot with water. That pot would sit on the stove or in the edge of the campfire and we drank it either hot or cold. When hot, we liked a little honey in it. He would dump it about every third day and start some more. We still use that tea.

In the early 30s, some marijuana was growing on the mountain and one of Daddy's Mexican goat herders was using it. Daddy came unglued. He fired the herder and pulled and destroyed all the plants. I have wondered how it got there. Did the herder plant it? Did the early Spanish plant it? Did the Indians plant it … or was it native? I don't suppose I'll ever know.

Chapter 7
Farming

Farming was never the big thing with us … we were ranchers. Daddy had some good ideas but they never panned out for some reason or other.

Water was the most important thing. When I was a kid, over by the *Russell Grove*, Daddy fixed a water hole for the cattle by just using a plow and a Fresno and four mules to dig a long trench down to the water, about 12 feet deep. The cattle could walk in from either end to get water. Now the farmers are pumping water from 350 feet or more.

In the 1920s and 1930s we got pretty good rains starting in July, for about three months. Daddy decided he could build a flood tank and have enough water to do some farming.

He got the flood tank started and cleared the mesquite off of 25 acres and he was ready to start his farm. For about two or three years we did pretty well. It was new ground and a lot of hard work but we raised a good crop of cattle feed and sweet corn. I don't remember clearing the land, but I do remember laying out the crop rows and making sure we kept them going downhill so the water would flow down to the end. If the water went too fast it would wash the seed out because the water couldn't sink in. The field wasn't very level so we had to go with the slope of the land to make the rows come out right.

We never had a tractor, so everything was done with mules. First we plowed the field, then harrowed it. The plow was the same one we used to loosen the dirt for the Fresno. The harrow was for breaking up the plowed soil ready for planting. Normally it was pulled by one mule, but Daddy fastened two together side by side and we used two mules. Daddy put a 1" x 12" board across them and I stood on the board and drove the mules. The harrow was a metal frame that had a bunch of metal teeth on the underside that could be adjusted by a big long handle on top to change depth and angle of the teeth.

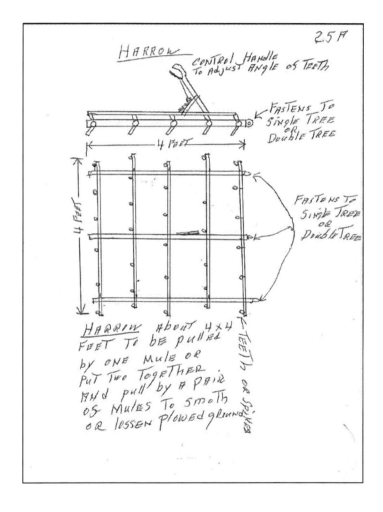

Daddy got me started with the mules, Buck and Billy, and I was going in a rectangular pattern, ever getting smaller toward the center. As the rectangle got smaller, my turns at the end got tighter until at the center I turned the corner too tight and turned the double harrow over on top of me. The big long handles kept it from smashing me but my foot got caught and Buck and Billy just kept going, dragging me under the harrow. I must have made some pretty loud noises, because Daddy came running and saved my bacon. I wasn't hurt, so we turned the harrow back over and I finished harrowing. I must have been nine or ten years old because it was before I got the Model T Ford.

Boy! Mom sure had a great garden and we did eat well. We had venison from the mountain and veggies from the garden. How could we eat any better?

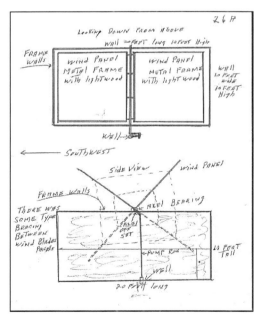

Then the rains got less and the crops didn't mature and all farming depended on pumping from underground water, so Daddy got another great idea, derived from pictures of wind pumps in Holland. He built a wind-powered pump.

The wind was almost always out of the southwest, and there was a lot of it, so he faced his pump accordingly.

It is hard for me to describe his pump so you might have to use your imagination to help me a little.

He had four walls forming a box. The ends were about 10' x 10' and the sides about 10' x 20'. On the top center of the 10' x 20' walls he put a bearing. On a 12' axle he put four big wooden paddle blades about 9' x 9'. By placing the axle into the bearings, the wind couldn't hit the lower blades so it just hit the top blades. It had plenty of power, with the offset on the end of the axle directly over the pump it made for a water source.

It worked great for light winds, but if the wind got up very high, it would pump the well down. Just not enough water in the well. The well was about 80 feet deep.

Next, he didn't have a system for controlling its speed, so when the wind really got to blowing, it would just run away with itself. Finally the wind just tore it up, so we didn't even get one good year out of it.

Old Time Well Rig

Daddy gave up on farming and tried to raise fish in the flood tank. Two years it did pretty good and we had thousands of little catfish, but then we didn't get any rain that summer and the flood tank dried up, so that was the end of the fish. For years the weather got drier and drier, but Mom had her garden and Daddy planted his corn patch, about two acres. Sometimes it did all right and sometimes it didn't.

The corn can't tassel unless water is available for irrigation, so here they are with a well rig of the day drilling for water. They got enough for ranch and home use but not enough for farming.

Mom and Dad with his corn starting to tassel.

Years later they got a good well, about 100 yards north of the house and over 200 feet deep, but by this time Daddy was getting too old to work the land, so he just raised his corn and Mom's garden. Dyar, my youngest brother, farmed it for a while. It was too small to be profitable, but it is a good home place.

Chapter 8
Goat Dairy

In the early 1930s, a couple of infants in *Deming* were intolerant of the available milk, so the parents drove out to the ranch (about 10 miles) to get Mom's breast milk. This only lasted a short time, until they discovered that goat milk was agreeable as well as human breast milk.

The lightbulb came on in Daddy's head. "A goat dairy!" He had a little bunch of goats at that time, but he started building up the size of his herd and the quality and quantity of milk production.

Daddy got three men from *Deming* to come out to the ranch to make adobes (bricks) to build his dairy barn. I remember those men digging a hole out about 30 yards north of where Dyar's house is now. To me it looked like so much fun!

They made this big hole … and they put water in it and rolled up their pantlegs, took off their shoes, got in there and started playing in that mud. Here came Daddy with an armful of straw he threw in that mud hole with those guys. They kept trying to stomp it under the mud, but by the time they got it all stomped under, Daddy would bring some more straw. They kept testing how thick the mud was and pretty soon I guess it was thick enough so each of the men got a shovel and they kept stomping in the mud, but they took a shovelful of that mud over to some forms Daddy had built out to the side.

It wasn't long until all the forms were full and the mud hole was almost empty. They made sure the mud was nice and smooth on top of the forms. A few days later, the men came back and took the forms off and—hey! There lay a big bunch of adobes.

They stacked those adobes in a certain way so they could breathe and get plenty of sun. Daddy said that was the curing or maturing stage. They kept repeating this process until—goodness!—they had a lot of stacks of adobes. While the adobes were maturing the men poured a cement pad.

Using this same mud as mortar, they put up a nice building. They put very strong rafters on it with boards on them. They put something on the boards to protect them (I think it was tar), then they put about four inches of that mud on it. Daddy's goat dairy was ready to go, but the market wasn't strong enough to support his dairy.

The dairy adobe was used for many things over the years. Papa and Granny lived in it for a while, it was a tack room, and Luther's and my winter bedroom. Later, sorta junk room, then Dyar's maintenance shop. It was well over 70 years old when Dyar removed it.

Daddy now had some fine milk goats, so had plenty of milk for home use. And then some. A real good goat could produce six quarts a day, most goats just three, but a good goat could feed a calf. Daddy could buy day-old bull calves from the dairy for $1.00 each, so guess what?—we raised calves on those goats. Daddy fixed feed stalls for the goats and we could lock their heads in, to hold them so the calves could nurse. We usually had 12 to 14 calves at a time. We had to get up early to take care of them before we went to school. We caught the bus about sunup so started our day pretty early just to repeat the process when we got home from school.

The calves were Jersey calves, not the best quality of meat and they weren't very big so it wasn't a very profitable endeavor.

A sideline to this was we had a mare that died in foal birth and we raised the colt on the goats. That became an outstanding horse—"Misty", Luther's horse.

I think the work of taking care of goats and so much real hands-on is the reason all my siblings hate goats so bad. Oh, I don't really like them, but I don't hate them. I sure do like goat meat and goat milk. The goat dairy didn't make it, but the attempt sure left its mark.

Ralph McDougal

My sister Nettie cartooned animals. She was not fond of billy goats!

The Goats. Those Damn Goats!

Daddy always kept some milk goats. The herd of goats varied in size (about a hundred head) over the years. But in hard times they really made survival possible, because we always had goat meat, goat milk, and with beans we never did go hungry. When Mom's garden was producing we really ate well.

Daddy would also butcher four or five goats then in the Model A Ford, take them to *Deming*, *Silver City*, *Hatch*, or up on the *Mimbres River* and sell them or trade them for most anything of value. Daddy was a very good trader.

One time Daddy took his trade goods (goat meat) to *Hatch* and he came back with 1300 lbs. of tomatoes. The farmer couldn't sell his tomatoes, and Daddy hadn't been very successful, so they just traded.

Boy did we scramble to get as many tomatoes as possible canned before they spoiled. We had canned tomatoes for a long time.

As I said earlier, we also suckled calves on the goats, and even a horse (Misty).

The goats were a survival item.

~ ~ ~

Why "damn" goats? We all had our turn at herding them, and they were sure ornery critters. It was hard to keep them together—they would try to scatter. A goat could live on a pasture where a cow would starve to death.

Normally we had a horse, mule, or donkey to ride while herding them, but during very dry times we couldn't afford to keep feed for a riding animal, so we herded them on foot. We were ready, lunch and canteen in hand. The goats would be let out of the corral at sunup and we would head for the mountain, about three miles east of the ranch house.

Even in dry times the goats could browse pretty well on the side of the mountain. We weren't expected to be back to the ranch with them until sundown. Some of the bigger, stronger goats wanted to get to the mountain in a hurry, so they would take off and we had to urge the stragglers to keep up. Our hope was that the leaders would find something to eat and would wait for us to catch up.

We usually carried a .22 rifle and a slingshot. With a slingshot, we could sling a rock 50 or 60 yards to get their attention to turn them, but usually we had to run and turn them. Those damn goats were sure aggravating.

During dry times the rabbit population got pretty thin, so the coyotes would start working on the goats. Of course we shot a few with our .22 rifle but that wasn't enough.

Daddy had a big wether (a castrated goat) that he put a harness on and fastened a muzzled dog to the harness of the wether, so the goat led the dog wherever he wanted to. The dog couldn't bite the goat but he could sure bark and scare off the coyotes. When conditions on the range were right, we could turn them loose and just be sure we fed and watered the dog daily. If the coyotes had plenty of rabbit to eat, we could let the goats loose without the dog.

When Daddy could manage, he would have a goat herder. Each of us kids got our turn at herding those stinky, ornery, damn goats, but they really were lifesavers.

Chapter 9
Mom was a very good cook!

Mom always tried to have something for us when we got in from school. When we got off the bus up at the road about 250 or 300 yards east of the house, we could often smell what she had for us. There was usually a breeze from the west. We could get to the house in a hurry. So many times it might be rolls or cinnamon rolls or a roast. You could never tell.

One day we followed the smell in and Mom had just opened the oven door and sat a roast on it. For some reason it seemed a little different. It was a white meat, very tender, sort of greasy, and a small bone structure. Boy was it good, but Mom wouldn't tell us what it was until we were finished eating. Porcupine!

That big old wood cook range was kind of what our lives centered around. One cold morning when Luther was pretty small, Mom had just taken a big pan of biscuits out of the oven and she had left the oven door open. Luther came running into the kitchen to get warm because the kitchen was the only room that had heat in it. Well, Luther just plopped his cute little bottom down on that oven door. Boy did he burn his butt! I can remember him screaming and Mom grabbing him up and rubbing butter on it.

Our breakfast usually consisted of biscuits, gravy, eggs, some kind of meat, milk, butter and honey. We worked hard and we could sure eat.

The Lord was always a part of our lives. Mom and Daddy saw to that. We kids always took turns saying the blessing and the one I remember most is: "For food, for shelter, and loving care, we give Thee gracious thanks. Amen."

~ ~ ~

Daddy had two or three men working for him one time and they made the comment that they didn't say a blessing before they ate. Daddy stood up and said, "This is our house, our table, and our food. If you are not thankful enough to ask that it be blessed then you can get up and get out of my house and hit the road." I don't know who suggested it but we sang, *There Shall Be Showers of Blessing* and there was no more static out of those men.

Mom had a very big job feeding all of us, so all of us kids had things to do to help her. Our dinnerware was very special. No two pieces were alike, but there was one big old thick cup that Nadine hated, so whoever was setting the table saw to it that Nadine got that cup.

Our kitchen was small and the furniture wasn't much, but my elder sister Nettie saw to it that etiquette was followed. Children sat up straight at the table, no elbows on the table, didn't talk with food in the mouth. When one asked for food, one would say "Please pass the food" and "Thank you" and we didn't slurp or chew with our mouths open. Nettie was very strict and we disliked it at the time, but oh my goodness, it was needed discipline as we got out in the world. In my life, I have been to some special banquets and I think Nettie was with me at each one.

We grew up eating lots of beans and I think we all liked them. There was always a big pot of beans on the stove and sometimes we added them to our breakfast when we were working especially hard.

Mom insisted that we wash our hands before preparing food and before we sat down at the table.

~ ~ ~

Our normal routine was to bathe on Saturday night, or before going to church, in a #3 wash tub in the kitchen. It started with about ½ tub of cold water and hot water was added as each person bathed.

The water had to be carried in and heated on Mom's big wood-burning range. Of course the girls got to bathe first. Each one of us got a clean washrag and we would wash down as far as possible then up as far as possible ... then we would wash possible.

We always seemed to have a bar of store-bought soap for bathing, but Mom made a lot of lye soap for laundry. Lye soap cleaned the clothes real well. She used bluing to make them white—in the last rinse water—and the clothes would be a beautiful shade of blue. The sunshine would bleach them out to a beautiful white. The family preferred store-bought soap for bathing because it smelled good, and lye soap was hard on the skin and didn't smell good.

Just outside the kitchen door on the washstand there was a wash pan, a bar of soap, a towel and a water bucket. If there was water in the bucket, we were lucky 'cause if there was no water in it—that meant it was our turn to fill it.

We usually had two sets of clothes, one set was school clothes. Sometimes we had two pairs of shoes.

I was asked about deodorant and I can't remember ever using it until I got in the military and I didn't like it much, so I didn't use it, and still don't. If I smell it is because I need to wash.

On a day-to-day basis, if we were going to town or school or something special, a wash pan with washrag and bar of soap was used. Sometimes we had hot water from Mom's teakettle, but usually the water was cold.

We didn't brush our teeth very often and when we did it was a little rag wrapped around our finger and dipped in some salt or salt-and-soda.

After nearly 90 years I still have over half of my teeth and still eat a pretty good meal.

Things must not have been too bad because I never had any of the childhood diseases. I didn't have a cavity in my teeth until I was stationed at *Kirtland Air Force Base* in 1959, at the age of 34.

Ralph McDougal

My stepdaughter, Patty Cleary, was married to a jockey for several years (man that rides a race horse during a race). I asked her about the deodorant thing and the goat with the horses. She said in breaking those high-strung, nervous horses that before approaching the horse, they would get some of that horse's fresh dung and wipe it on their clothes. That smell was familiar to the horse and made them much more acceptable to the horse, but her husband wasn't to her. She had to put up with the smell until they got home from the stable and then she had to wash those clothes.

I asked Duane Pertle, Delah's cousin, what he used as a deodorant, and he said, "I didn't use any until I was riding in the rodeo circuit during the 1940s. Here we were ... big young cowboys competing with each other to see who could ride the worst bronc. We wanted to be as tough as the bronc and wanted to smell like the bronc, so we used a road apple (horse turd) and rubbed it under our arms and so on. We smelled the part of being a real cowboy." Duane told this as the truth and I don't doubt it.

Patty said most people kept a goat with their horses, but her husband kept a rooster with his. She said that rooster and horse were almost inseparable, apart only during a race. That was the cutest little banty rooster. He had feathers all the way down to his feet, a beautiful comb, and fancy tail—his tail feathers were gorgeous. He would fly up and sit on the horse's head.

Chapter 10
Grandpa—"Little Matt" (McDougal)

I don't know how long Grandpa spent in the *Alamogordo* area, but it was a big part of the late 1800s. Grandpa was born in *Neosho, Missouri*. He had trouble with the law and escaped to *White Oaks, New Mexico*, near *Carrizozo, New Mexico*.

A lady hotel owner there took him in and he helped with the hotel. He went on to *La Luz, New Mexico*, where outlaws hung out—*La Luz* was up in the canyon then, but now it's below the mouth of the canyon where the farm land is better. Also, it is now an artists' community.

Grandpa was living in *La Luz* when he met Nettie Shely. She sang and played tambourine and her cousin played the organ while Reverend Shely preached. She went with Grandpa McDougal and stayed awhile—when they got back Reverend Shely insisted they get married. They lived there in *La Luz* and my daddy was born there.

Grandpa worked for Oliver Lee. Colonel Fountain was the judge to try Oliver Lee's case. The trial was to take place in *Mesilla* (near where *Las Cruces, New Mexico,* is now), but on his trip from *Alamogordo* to *Las Cruces*, he disappeared. Oliver Lee was suspect, so he left the country. He had horses and cattle on his ranch—a huge ranch—and Grandpa took care of it while he was gone. Grandpa was Oliver Lee's right-hand man, or bodyguard (gunman), along with another man. Grandpa was called "Little Matt".

Ralph McDougal

When Oliver Lee came back and gave himself up (late 1800s), he told Grandpa to take his family and get out of the country, that he didn't need to get mixed up in it. I was never told what really happened. That is when they moved down near *San Antonio, Texas.*

The Oliver Lee Ranch Headquarters is now a New Mexico State Memorial. (See the well-researched book; *The Two Alberts: Fountain and Fall* by Gordon R. Owen, 1996.)

Down in *San Antonio*, Grandpa had a good thing going (according to Daddy), a good farm and ranch. They had a field of corn, and the next rancher's cattle kept getting into it. Grandpa accused the rancher of cutting the fence. The next time they got into the corn, Grandpa sent the boys down to put them out and to show no mercy.

I guess they roughed those cows up pretty good because the rancher sent word that if it happened again Grandpa needed to strap on his hogleg (a six-shooter) because he would be coming after him. It happened again and each man with his hogleg met somewhere between the ranches and went for their gun. The rancher was hit in the hip and knocked off his horse but Grandpa wasn't hit. Grandpa said he needed to finish the job so he rode up beside him and shot him again.

That shooting set off a long series of events. Grandpa went back to the house and got a black stallion that they were very proud of and headed west for *New Mexico Territory*–not yet a state, and Texas lawmen could not come after him. He said he was traveling fast. He would travel all night and hole up in the daytime because of the wolves. This is when I realized that I was the offspring of an outlaw hiding in the *New Mexico Territory*.

I don't know why he stopped in the *Little Floridas* near *Deming, New Mexico*, but he found a cave in the north end of the mountain that he lived in for about two years. After he had been there a short while, he got word to Grandma Nettie and the family—Alva, Artie, Hamp, Sue, Noble, and Jim—to ship their cattle to *El Paso* by train and they could come on up and join him. They had about 300 head of beef cattle and several milk cows. The steers all died of shipping fever but some of the milk cows made it. After losing so much, the family settled in *Ysleta* just below *El Paso*, *Texas*, and the boys peddled milk to get by until Grandpa could get ready for them.

What is now the *Two Spear Ranch* started in 1902 as Hamp McDougal's (my dad) homestead. Little Matt McDougal, (Grandpa the outlaw) homesteaded just west of us when the Taylor Grazing Act came out in 1933. Homesteaders were granted the land they'd been grazing, so Daddy got the whole mountain. He started with his homestead and as homesteaders around would give up, Dad would buy their land for $.03 to $.05 cents an acre, just enough for a train ticket home.

The family grew up scattered from *Maine* to *California* where they still are, and Nadine has ended up with the *Two Spears Ranch* after many years of hard work.

When Daddy was staying with us in about 1969, he took us up to *La Luz* and showed us where he was born. At the time of his birth, the town of *La Luz* was up in a little box canyon about a mile east of where it is now.

The House Location in La Luz.

Their house was on a little red hill in this box canyon. When they put the road in they used that little red hill as fill dirt for the road.

Grandpa had a soft spot for people. He would often bring in a deer or wild turkey for the families that were having a hard time. One time as he was coming home down *Alamo Canyon*, he spotted some turkeys still on the roost, so he decided to try his skill with his side arm and he shot three turkeys before they could get off the roost. He dressed the turkeys and put all three gizzards in one of the turkeys. Well, the family he gave that turkey to called him 'the man who shot the turkey with three gizzards'.

Chapter 11
Sleepy Grass

Daddy told a story on Grandpa, about Sleepy Grass.

Oliver Lee's ranch took in about the whole country and they raised cattle and horses. Grandpa took care of the horses along with other things. He would round up his young horses and put them in on the Sleepy Grass for a few days and then sell or trade them as gentle horses. Of course when they got off the Sleepy Grass they would come unwound. They weren't gentle at all. The Sleepy Grass is now a forest service picnic and camping ground.

While staying at *Oliver Lee State Park*, Delah and I got pictures of Oliver Lee ranch headquarters, the homesite in *La Luz*, the Sleepy Grass, and family grave sites in *Alamogordo*.

Grandpa was a very serious person, and his language was foul—
he could cuss like a sailor … he used it pretty often. He did not
smoke. His speech was very clear, he spoke well. In my memory he
always wore a suit with vest and tie, and he could draw all kinds of
things out of those vest pockets. Working or going to town, this is the
way I remember him. I can't remember his sense of humor. He was
very verbal on politics. I don't remember anything about education,
or family of origin.

As for skills, Grandpa could do just about anything. He had a high
opinion of himself—if the boys couldn't do it, well by God he could!

He wasn't hairy, he wasn't smelly, he was a clean-shaven person
and I never remember him smelling bad. Grandpa lived in the house
with us. I don't know that he had any women friends. He was
respected and loved and liked and could tell good stories. We were
real close. He was a little man, only 5'2" and didn't weigh a hundred
pounds until after he was sixty years old. He'd always have chickens
or turkeys or something to work with. He wore a truss all the time—
he had roped a steer to show his boys how to do it. The horse fell and
the saddle horn went into him. The truss kept his insides in.

Grandpa's big thing was kerosene—kerosene would cure
anything. Some cats had ticks in their ears, and he dipped them in
kerosene…all 13 got it in their ears and went crazy. I shot 13 cats.
When we got a cold or sore throat, he would fix a sugar tit (cloth with
sugar tied in it) and put a few drops of kerosene in it. If you got a
scratch or cut—put kerosene on it. Later we had iodine, but that was
his cure. "Us kids" always thought he was just about it, and Daddy
did too. He was always right in the middle of everything.

When he was 69 years old, Grandpa bought a Model T. It was a
real buy for him, less than $400. Of course he didn't know how to
drive it, but he wanted to go to *California* to see the pretty girls on the
beach. So Uncle Noble and Uncle Jim drove him to *California*. Uncle
Artie lived in *California* at the time. This is hearsay because it was

before my time, but I do remember my uncles teasing him about being so old that he couldn't do anything about it if he caught one of those pretty girls.

~ ~ ~

Our nice house had burned—according to my sisters it was nice—and the ranch kitchen was our whole house. It had a dirt floor. Grandpa didn't drink or chew, but he spit—he often cleared his throat and spit. He thought it was perfectly fine for him to spit on the dirt floor, but he and Mom had some rows over that when she'd get on him. I think they usually got along great, but she didn't like him spitting on the floor!

A few years before Grandpa died, a couple of officers came up to the ranch from *El Paso* to see him. They wanted him to clear his conscience and he told them to go to hell, he never killed a man that didn't need killing. I remember this happening.

He is buried in *Deming*, as well as Granny and Papa Toney.

Chapter 12
Grandpa's Hideout

Grandpa's hideout from *Indian Wells Rock*—To get up to the hideout, start by going into the big crack in the lower left corner of the picture and climb up to the left side of the little clump of trees.

Then go behind the big rock on the left of the tree, then do a sharp right and climb up the crack to the hideout. This last part gets pretty tricky. I did it at 87. From the kitchen, one can go out over the top to the *North Trail* but it is a long way around.

Grandpa's hideout had a living room, bedroom, and kitchen. Some of the living room ceiling has fallen in and brush has grown up. Living room is about 12 to 15 feet across, 6 to 7 foot ceiling. The bed chamber has just enough room for a 1-man bed, a hole in the side of the bluff about 6' x 3'. The kitchen is about 3' x 15', long and narrow, with a lot of brush grown up in it.

The first 8' or 10' is open on top. Small trees have grown up in the passageway to the cooking area. Bluff line is 50' to 60' high. His water supply was a seep that came over the bluff about 50 yards west of the hideout, and it ran down into a pool that was kind of in the bluff about the size of a bathtub. There was water in it most of the year before I went into the service. Small animals, bees, etc. watered there all the time. That was the Indians' water supply, and there was an Indian work area in the bluff on the west between the watering hole and *Indian Grind Rock.*

Indian Grind Rock

Indian Grind Rock is a huge rock just below the bluff, with about eleven grind holes in it. So the Indians must have used it a long time judging from the depth of the holes.

Ralph McDougal

A side view of Indian Grind Rock

Grandpa's hideout, about a mile away.

Chapter 13
Grandma Nettie

What I know about Grandma Nettie isn't very much. She died rather young so I never did know her. I have seen her picture and she was certainly a very beautiful Spanish woman.

From what Daddy and Grandpa told me, Grandpa met her in *La Luz, New Mexico*, in the latter part of the 1800s. She and her dad, Reverend Shely, and her cousin were preaching to the *Mescalero Indians*. They had a wagon to live in and haul the foot-pedaled organ. Her cousin played the organ and sang and Grandma Nettie had a tambourine and sang and my great-grandfather, Reverend Shely preached to the Indians and I guess anybody else that would listen.

He was preaching to the Indians, his son-in-law was an outlaw, and part

*Great-grandfather
Reverend Warren Shely*

of his family was in the *Texas Rangers*.

Ralph McDougal

WARREN O. SHELY, Father of Nettie Shely McDougal
Circuit Rider for Methodist Church

Grandma Nettie's mother was a Spanish woman whose family owned the *Benavidas Land Grant* near *San Antonio, Texas*, that was issued by *Spain*. How Miss Benavidas and Reverend Shely got together I have no idea. She died at Grandma Nettie's birth.

Over the years, Grandma Nettie received several rather large sums of money which set her up pretty good in *Deming*. Grandpa didn't prove to be the best of husbands and would go through money in a hurry. In later years, Grandpa and Grandma Nettie were estranged, with Grandpa living at the ranch and Grandma Nettie living in *Deming*. It seems Grandpa was sorta wild and rough and Grandma Nettie was more refined. We understand that Grandma Nettie's family, the Shelys, had a number of *Texas Rangers*.

Grandma Nettie died in 1912 at the age of 39, but she sure left a fine family. Grandpa (Little Matt) and Grandma Nettie had six children—five boys and a girl: Alvie, Artie, Hamp, Sue, Noble and Jim. We are putting down a very brief account of the offspring of one of those children—Luther H. McDougal (Hamp), my dad, son of one of the "Old West Outlaws" in the *New Mexico Territory*.

Granny and Papa Toney.

Loney Longest Toney was a descendent of the Nashes from *Nashville, Tennessee.*

She married Papa Toney when she was fifteen and he was thirty.

Granny was a large woman. I don't think of her as fat, but heavy-busted. Matter-of-fact, I don't think of her being shapely at all, or of her as a pretty woman, but she was very pleasant to us kids.

I remember her with a smile on her face. She said things exactly as she saw them, and they were comical. To me she was a positive person, we couldn't be around her without having a smile on our faces. She was an outgoing type of a person, and Papa Toney wasn't.

Papa Toney, his father and two of his brothers had a wagon train that operated between *St. Joseph, Missouri*, and *Vale, Oregon*. Mom and most of her siblings were born in *Vale, Oregon*. Mom said they didn't very often go to town (*Boise, Idaho*) because they had to swim the *Snake River*. She said they had a big, gentle horse they called the kids' horse. To cross the *Snake* they would tie a rope to the saddle horn and tie knots in it for the kids to hold onto and that horse would take them across.

~ ~ ~

Ralph McDougal

When the railroad was completed across the U.S., it put the wagon train out of business. By this time Papa and Granny had a pretty good-sized family and so they headed out in a covered wagon looking for work. They heard there was work in southern *New Mexico*.

It took them several years, working at small jobs along the way, to get to *New Mexico*. Papa Toney worked as carpenter, ore wagon driver, and ranch hand—just about anything he could find. They were in *Old Town*, *New Mexico*, when Daddy and Mom met. *Old Town* is now a ghost town halfway between *Deming* and *Silver City*, *New Mexico*. Papa Toney got a good job as a carpenter at *Ft. Bayard Army Base*, *New Mexico*.

Kids were to be seen and not heard. As a result, Papa Toney wasn't involved with us kids. He sat and read his paper and smoked his cigarettes. But if you had a question about current events, he would be the one to be up-to-date on it.

Papa Toney sat in a captain's chair, kind of slouched down, with his left leg crossed over his right; his arms resting on the arms of the chair, holding his paper up in front of him and wore big metal-rim glasses. He rolled his own smokes and had a cigarette in his mouth with smoke curling up. He had a white mustache with yellow stains on the upper right side. He didn't talk unless you talked to him; he didn't offer anything at all. He was a carpenter and handyman at *Ft. Bayard*, an army base with a hospital (where Muriel, Nadine and I were born).

We went up to *Ft. Bayard* some when Papa Toney was working there. Later they took the old Morgan homestead (one of the homesteads my dad purchased for 5 cents an acre) moved the building and built a little house up close to where Dyar and Nadine's mailboxes are now. They had some cattle that ran on the ranch that we took care of. Their little house was later moved over to a spot on the east side of the ranch house. It is now setting on the west side of Dyar's pond. They lived in the adobe for some time also.

About all I can remember about Papa Toney was him sitting reading and smoking. He'd sit by the hour, read and smoke. I don't know that Grandpa McDougal and Papa Toney ever crossed paths. Granny and Papa Toney lived in a little house of their own.

Now Granny Toney was something else. She said it just like it was, she pulled no punches. When Granny got her first Social Security check of $23 we thought she was rich. She bought a big steak and Mom fixed it for her and "us kids" all got a bite of that steak. She said, "Now this is a real steak!"

Papa Toney and Granny were there but I had very little interaction with them.

Chapter 14
My First Car

I was always very fond of turkeys, so for my 11th birthday my mom bought me twelve day-old turkeys. By fall my turkeys were really pretty. I had eight of them left, which was about the normal loss of little chickens or turkeys.

Grandpa kept trying to trade me out of them. He had a 1923 Model T Ford that had been sitting for some time with flat tires and looked pretty bad. Grandpa had never learned to drive. He wanted to trade me that car for my turkeys.

I asked Daddy about it, and he said, "Ralph, this is your deal. Not mine." I finally traded Grandpa my eight turkeys for his 1923 Model T Ford, a pocket knife, and 50 cents. I now owned my first car at the age of 11. What a car! It was then a big part of our lives. By the way, a Model T is a very different breed. The 'T' does not have to have a battery. It runs by magnetos. A battery is a luxury.

In a sense, it was a convertible. It had 4-cylinders, 30" x 3.5" tires with tubes 50 psi, and wooden spoke wheels. The throttle was a fingertip lever beneath the right side of the steering wheel. Spark advance control was the same type lever under the left side of the steering wheel. It had a bench seat in front and a bench seat in back and three doors—there was no door for the driver because that is where the high gear lever is. On the floor at the base of the steering column were three foot pedals.

With high gear lever standing straight up, push the spark lever all the way up and the throttle lever down just a little. Pull the choke out and then go out in front and start cranking. CAUTION: Hold the crank with fingers and thumb on the same side of the crank handle to prevent a broken hand or arm. When it starts, rush around and adjust spark, throttle and choke to keep it running.

When it is running good, to go forward give it a little throttle and press down on the low gear pedal till it gets to moving good then give it a little more throttle and let up on the low gear pedal and push the high gear lever down at the same time and it is rolling along. As speed is increased, also advance the spark. When the brake is applied, it stops the drive shaft which stops the rear wheels. The front wheels don't have any brakes. If for some reason the brakes don't work, use the reverse pedal.

It didn't have a water pump, just a radiator fan. It didn't have a fuel pump—gravity feed. It didn't have an oil pump. It had a rod cap/dip system. Top speed was about 35 mph and it didn't have a speedometer. We got about 22 mpg. It had springs but no shocks. Each spark plug had its own coil with open points. The coil had a little nut to adjust the points and we adjusted them by their buzzing sound.

Boy it was a lot of fun and we sure did use it!

On cold days we would build a fire and push the Model T up until the oil pan was right over the fire. It started a lot easier that way. Sometimes we would use a horse to pull-start it, other times we might have enough kids to push-start it.

When I got the Model T, Daddy said, "I'll tell and show you how to work on it, but I will not touch it."

Luther and I got so we were good at tire repair and we could put new bands in the transmission beside the road in pretty short order. Of course we couldn't afford to buy new bands, but a fabric GI belt was just the right size. And Daddy got us some from someplace. He got a lot of them and we used a lot of them because they weren't as tough as the real bands. We busted a piston on the Model T, so we took one out of the 1927 Model T that Mark Terry gave us. But guess what—it was aluminum and ours was cast iron. But it worked fine in number 4 position from then on.

We got to where we could take down and overhaul the Model A (the family car), the washing machine engine, and the pump jack engine. We even drew up plans to make a tractor out of a Model A, a truck rear end, and double transmissions. I left for the service before we got it done, but Luther and Dyar finished it. And they said it worked pretty well.

Luther and I installed pulleys on the blades of the windmill to run a generator for electric lights, but I left before we got that finished. They never finished that project.

Luther and I got to where an electric shock didn't bother us much. We could grab hold of all four spark plugs on that old Model T and kill the engine. There was a reason we could do that. Daddy took a Model T coil and made an electric fence to go around the field so he could put a few sheep in there.

His sheep, being the dumbest animals in the world, would hit that wire, and instead of backing off they would just lay down on the wire and bawl. To shut it off we'd have to go clear back up to the house. So we got to where we would just grab the sheep, shock and all, and pull it off the wire. (But I couldn't take it very well when Nadine grabbed my ear! as you'll soon learn.) This served me well in electronics, because to see if something was hot, I'd stick my finger to it to see if it had electricity (unless it was high voltage—and most electronics are low voltage).

~ ~ ~

We (Nadine, Luther and Dyar and myself) were going over just southwest of Cody's place where some people had some four-legged chickens. They had four legs, but the front ones were very small and fit up close to their breast. Interesting.

On the way home we went through a pretty big draw with sand in the bottom and I stalled out with my front wheels up on the bank and my rear wheels down in the draw. We worked our little tails off trying to start the car but with no luck.

A Cowboy Goes to War

I walked to the house to ask Daddy to tell us what to do. He told me he wouldn't touch my Model T, but he would tell me how to work on it. Well, all we had to do was to push it until the back wheels were as high as the front wheels. The gas was gravity feed, so if we were low on gas, which was always the case, we had to watch it when we came to a steep place. Simple! Just turn around and back up the hill.

We also learned that if we would get it warmed up on gasoline, we could switch to Mom's coal oil and it would do pretty good. Gas was more expensive than coal oil. Gas was 18 cents a gallon and coal oil was only six cents a gallon.

Daddy traded for a horse down by the Sunshine School and asked "us kids" to go get him, so Nadine, Luther, Dyar and I put saddle, bridle, and a 5-gallon can of water in the Model T and headed out.

The 5-gallon can of water? Yes, the 1923 Model T was before they put water pumps on them. If we drove really slow, we could get by okay. But no way could we stand to drive that slow, so we took extra water and looked like a steam engine going along. Eventually we'd run out of water. Boy, when we ran out of water and peed in the radiator it sure did stink!

We got the horse and headed home, with Luther riding the horse and me driving the Model T. Nadine and Dyar were with me, and we were so happy with our car. The horse was a big horse and had been a good horse, but he was old and looked like a nag. But he was going along pretty good. Luther said, "I'll race you!" and I said, "Okay. We will wait for you up at the corner." And off we went. You know what? Luther was waiting for us at the corner, that old nag could outrun us.

Before we stripped it down, Luther and I ran a wire from one of the coils to a switch under the dash and then through the length of the back seat. Boy, we sure got some response with that! But Nadine soon got to ride in the front seat, because she would sit on the wire and grab my ear to ground it.

That sure got my attention.

Ralph McDougal

~ ~ ~

We were using the Model T to wrangle horses, but there were two drawbacks. It was too slow, and it got too many flats.   We took the body off of it to lighten it, and put a very small pickup-type bed on it. We sat on the gas tank to drive it.

Mark Terry gave us a 1927 Model T that had been wrecked, so we used it for spare parts. The '27 had balloon tires on it, 4.5 x 21, mine had 30 x 3.5. Mine took 50 lbs. of air pressure, and the balloon tires only took 35 psi. Well, we changed out the right rear wheel to the balloon tire and ran it that way for some time, but then got balloon tires on both rear wheels.

To stop having so much trouble with mesquite thorns, we would pick up the right size tires along the highway and cut the bead out of them. We then let the air out of our tires and forced the acquired tire over it and aired it up again. We would keep the air pressure low so there was a little slippage between the two tires, and that helped by breaking the thorns off between the two tires.

With this setup it took a very fast horse to outrun us, and we had a lot less trouble with flats.

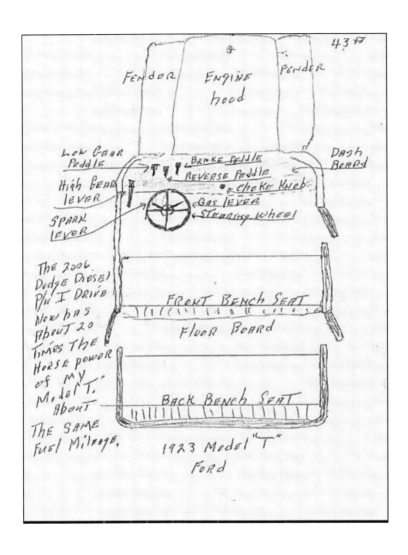

43 ₸

FENDER   ENGINE   FENDER
          hood

Low Gear   BRAKE PEDDLE   Dash
Peddle   REVERSE PEDDLE   Board

High Gear   • CHoKe Kneb.
lEVER   GAS lEVER

SPARK   ← STEERING WHEEL
lEVER

The 2006.
Dodge Diesel
P/u I Drive
Now has
About 20   FRoNT BENch SEAT
TiMes The
Horse power   FlooR BoARd
of MY
Model T.
About   BAck BENch SEAT
The SAME
Fuel Mileage.   1923 Model "T"
                 FoRd

Chapter 15
Life on the Ranch

Pump Jack

Water was the key to life on the ranch. We depended on the windmill. But when the wind didn't blow, we used the pump jack and the pump jack engine. When the pump jack engine failed and was beyond repair, we still had to have water, so "us kids" climbed up on the windmill platform and turned the windmill blade by hand, taking turns. But we didn't like that at all so we figured out how to use the Model T as a pump jack engine.

The pump jack engine is a little one-cylinder engine with an exterior piston rod and it was lubricated with a little grease cup.

It had two big fly wheels that we could use to start it with. With the drive belt off, we set the carburetor on choke, grabbed the fly wheels, and turned them as fast as possible.

When the engine starts, re-adjust the carb for desired running speed. Next slip the drive belt onto the flywheel pulley very carefully not to get a finger caught in it. Now adjust the carb for proper sucker rod speed. The drive belt transfers the power from engine to the pump jack pulley which is geared down to the pump jack lift wheel. The lift wheel is connected to the sucker rod by the sucker rod arm. As the pump jack lift wheel turns clockwise, it will cause the lift stroke to be almost perpendicular and thereby cause less wear of the sucker rod against the well pipe.

The engine has two flywheels with a drive belt pulley on only one of them. The pump jack and engine have a lot of bearings on them, open piston rod bearing, open crank shaft bearings, and piston lubricating oil in gas.

Cooling is a water jacket around the piston cylinder. All of the open bearings were lubricated with a grease cup. A grease cup held about an ounce with inside threads, grease cup cover fitting outside threads, crank shaft, and crank shaft bearing cap. Fill the grease cup with grease and screw the cover onto the grease cup until snug. That would push grease down around the crank shaft. Each time before starting, we had to be sure the grease cup was full and then give it about a quarter turn.

In all, there were about seven grease cups on the system. We made sure the water jacket was full and that the gas had the right amount of oil in it. Now we were ready to crank it by turning the flywheels. Sometimes all goes right and we could leave it until it ran out of gas.

In early summer it got so dry with not a breath of air. Well, Mom's garden and the stock needed water but with no wind blowing to turn the windmill, no water came up out of the well. The pump jack engine was beyond repair. Luther and I built a ramp so we could set the right rear wheel of the Model T on the pump jack pulley and block it down good and tie the left rear wheel down solid.

Just at idle the Model T could sure pump water, but after a bit it would get hot. To fix that, we stuck a hose up the discharge pipe of the pump and ran it over to the radiator of the Model T. We ran a return from the drain plug over to the dirt tank, and that little old Ford ran nice and cool and so did we. No more pumping water by hand, and for some reason we had no trouble getting gas. We couldn't afford the 18 cents a gallon. But pumping water for the stock and Mom's garden—hey! They furnished the gas.

Home Life

Luther and Dyar and I never had a room to sleep in. I slept on the little south porch with Grandpa. When I was about 13 and Grandpa was about 84, they moved him into town to live with Aunt Sue. He was my buddy. He didn't live long after he moved to town. Oh, I did miss Grandpa. So I decided to move out to the saddle shop in the adobe. Luther moved with me.

~ ~ ~

In the spring we got a steel military bed frame and hung it under a limb in the big cottonwood with chains. Luther and I slept on the same bed—big enough for two people. It was a single military cot—made out of angle iron 6'2" long and 36" wide and it had flat wire on the bottom and springs in each end and two or three springs on each side. It had about a three-inch GI cotton mattress. It would hold a pretty good weight. Between us we might weigh as much as a normal man.

Making up our bed in the morning was pulling a tarp up over it to keep the birds from messing in it. We had to strap it down so it wouldn't blow off and we dropped a rope over the side to climb up to bed. We climbed hand over hand up that rope in a hurry. That worked pretty well for a while, but if there was much of a wind, I would get air sick and throw up and fill my shoes down below. We changed the location of the frame to the forks of the tree, and it was much more stable. Sometime in December we would move back into the adobe saddle shop till sometime in March.

We got the idea of a fun way to come down out of our nest. We tied a cable to a limb up above our bed and stretched it to a post across the parking area. We made some hand holds on a pulley and hung it over the cable, and we were ready. Well, I was older and kind of the boss, so I headed down that cable … and it sure went fast. But our calculations were a bit off. We'd stretched the cable a little too tight and tied it too high on the post. I had no way of slowing down before I hit the post. Hit it I did! Luther is still laughing, but I didn't laugh. I slept in the tree until I went into the service, and I think Luther and Dyar did until they got out of high school. The big cottonwood tree died in the spring of 2012.

Daddy made us take the cable down because it got in the way of parking.

When we had kids come to spend the night, Mom would give us a GI blanket and tell us to go play Indian. A GI blanket is a rough wool army blanket, very warm. When Mom gave us the GI blanket, it wasn't that old "ugly green blanket". It was that "Army Olive Drab Blanket." (GI = Government Issue.)

While on Indians: there was an old man Sims who stayed with us some early on. He never took his hat off. To Mom, we never went outside without a hat, and we never wore our hat in the house, which was the way of the West. Well, Old Man Sims never took his hat off and that bothered me. So Daddy said, "Oh, he was scalped by the Indians," and left it at that.

Old Man Sims was chopping some wood for Mom, and I was carrying it in. A little dust devil came along and blew his hat off, and boy he grabbed his head and put on a show. I never knew whether the show was for my benefit, or if it really hurt that much.

I always thought that an Indian took the whole scalp. With Old Man Sims, they only took a patch about the size of one of Mom's biscuits, about 2½ inches in diameter.

As I remember, it looked just like a membrane—real pink color— it wasn't shiny smooth but like little blood vessel lines in it. Remember, I'm telling this from 80 years ago.

~ ~ ~

Times were hard at the ranch. Beans were our staple food. I remember you could buy split beans for animal feed. After dried, beans were mechanically cleaned, the whole beans were sold for human food and the halves for animals. We would buy the halves for food. Split beans made a delicious, hearty bean soup.

We never had electricity on the ranch while I lived there; we used coal oil lamps. When Daddy went to work in *El Paso* with a little money coming in, he had a carbide system put in to have gas lights. It didn't last too long 'cause it was too expensive, but it made its mark.

There was a big tank buried in the back yard and we would put carbide and water in it and it would mix them as needed to furnish gas for the lights in the house, and it was nice. One of the points that sold Daddy on the system was a good white wash. So we kids got to play Tom Sawyer and whitewash everything on the place.

While Daddy was still working in *El Paso*, he came home one weekend and there was a bunch there for dinner. Mom called for someone to get her some wood for her big range, she called two or three times and everyone ignored her. Pretty soon she called again and said dinner was ready. When we got in there it was nice and cool and we knew something was wrong. Yep, the food was all on the table but it was uncooked. Not much was said, but she soon had plenty of wood.

Before Daddy went back to work that time, I got a lesson in how to handle dynamite. I had been with him some when we had used it. Well, I had instruction to go up on the side of the mountain above where Nadine's house is now, and take out some of those big cedar stumps.

Okay—Nadine, Dyar and I got in the Model T with tools, ropes, and chains, and headed for the mountain. Luther brought up a couple of horses. When we decided on a stump, we would dig a hole under it on the uphill side and proceed to put a charge of dynamite in it.

Nadine carried the caps, the fuse, and the dynamite. I would take a stick of dynamite, then I would cut off (Daddy said) "four inches" of fuse, so I wouldn't tarry, but my four inches sometimes got a bit longer than four inches. Next I would insert the fuse into the cap and would crimp it with my teeth. Daddy said I would be more careful than if I used a tool. Then insert it in the dynamite. I would then go put it in the hole under the stump and tamp it good. A fuse burns about an inch per second. I would be sure that Nadine, Luther and Dyar were well hidden behind some rocks, and I would light the fuse. I'll bet I set a record getting behind the rocks with the crew. A quarter stick would normally just break the stump loose without tearing it up.

One time, as soon as I got behind the rocks, I looked back and Daddy's black and tan hound—Sport, was lying in the shade on the opposite side of the stump from the charge. About that time the charge went off and the picture in my mind is of that dog in midair, running like hell as they do in the cartoons. He didn't stay with us. He headed for the house! No, he wasn't hurt.

Then the work began. We tied a trace chain around the stump and it had a swivel in it so it wouldn't twist up our rope. We would tie our rope to the chain to drag the stump down to the Model T. The horse we liked for that was Dexter, he was pretty big and very quick. That was good because sometimes when a stump broke loose you needed to get out of the way and get loose from it, and let it go on down the hill.

The Model T wouldn't carry but two or three of these stumps. To load those stumps which were much bigger than we were, we had to roll them. If that didn't work, Luther would pull with Dexter while the rest of us pushed. When we got to the house, Sport the hound came to meet us as if to say he forgave us.

~   ~   ~

Alda was the firstborn and what a brilliant person! Daddy worked her on the ranch like the boy he wanted. She broke horses and did it all. She went on to be a well-known artist, a metallurgist, a college professor, and on and on. What she did for the rest of her sisters, brothers, and cousins was to set a standard that the rest of us were supposed to live up to. Well I don't think any of us ever did, but it was held out in front of us like a rabbit in front of the dogs on a racetrack.

~ ~ ~

We met a woman who was what we called a Holy Roller and after seeing her in action I wanted no part of that. To see her rolling around on the floor speaking in unknown tongues like she's off her rocker— I didn't want anything to do with it.

We attended the Seventh-day Adventist church with the Sincomb family in the little building by the old highway below *Lewis Flats*. I guess that is where I got my basic religious education. The little house we went to church in is still there, but it is pretty run-down.

We were raised as a God-fearing family.

~ ~ ~

Old Number 9 was a fair-sized black mule with long ears and a white nose. He was a good work mule, strong and steady.

Daddy had me cleaning the manure out of the goat and sheep pens and putting it on the two-acre field north of the house. The manure was a foot deep or more and was packed pretty hard, so I was using a slip scraper and old Number 9. The slip scraper had a sharp blade and if you work it just right it would pick up the manure. So in a circle we would go, pens to field and back again.

The slip scraper had two handles on it and it took both hands to load it or dump it.

So the reins (lines) were tied together and put across my shoulders so I was controlling the mule by shoulder movement and talking to him. Now remember, the mule has a blind bridle on, so he can't see what is going on behind him.

At that time we had a bunch of pigeons, and they like salt. We had salt in the pens for the livestock. My circle with old Number 9 went right by the salt. Number 9 and I had just passed the salt when that entire flock of pigeons swooped down to the salt with a loud swoosh, and Number 9 thought his world was coming to an end. And he decided he needed to get out of there.

Boy, all hell broke loose. He squealed and started kicking and bucking and running. I had both hands on the slip scraper and the reins over my shoulders, so he jerked me down and the handles didn't help much. Number 9 flat ran away with that slip scraper and it was just hitting the ground and bouncing. I got a horse to go after Number 9 and found parts of the slip scraper and single tree for a half mile into the north pasture. When I got to him, Number 9 was calm and acting as if nothing had happened. He and I gathered things up on the way back and were soon making our circle again.

To load the slip scraper, lift up on the handles until the blade starts cutting and it will fill the scraper. (About three or four wheelbarrow loads). To dump, lift the handles up sharply and the blade will catch and pull the scraper on over. To get ready for the next load, walk up beside it and jerk it back quickly so the blade doesn't catch, and it is ready for another load.

~ ~ ~

When Daddy was working in *El Paso* and Luther and I were riding the ranch a lot and many of our nights were up at the big gap, we had a neat little dog called Coley. Coley was a cocker spaniel and she was coal black. Whatever Luther and I were doing, she was right in the middle of it. She stayed with us while we were riding and when we got to cutting cattle or running horses, she couldn't keep up. I would stop and she would rear up with her front feet on my stirrup and I would reach down and pick her up by the front feet and set her in the saddle in front of me and she could ride as good as I could.

She got to looking very thin and sore-footed. Daddy said, "Boys, that is cruel. She is too small to keep up that pace." He thought we should have a hound. When Daddy went back down to *El Paso* he took her with him and gave her away.

We were some upset but we got over it. But she's got a place in my heart—she was our dog, our companion. And even today when I think of it—nostalgia—it was a happy moment in life with a sad ending.

~ ~ ~

In about 1939 when the water was gone on top of the mountain, we went up to bring the cattle and horses down. Well, when we got everything gathered, Inky was missing. Inky was a little black mare and she was very old. We figured she had gone off somewhere and died, so we didn't bother spending much time looking for her.

The next season when we took the stock back up on top, lo and behold there was Inky with a beautiful horse colt. He was kind of a blue-gray color with long mane and tail. I guess she spent her time in *Mamie Canyon*. There is a little rock water hole that is very hard to get to, but I guess she did.

Daddy said, "Well Ralph, you found them so I guess that colt is yours." I was about 15. That sure tickled me and I named him Majesty.

We left them in the mountain until Majesty was a long two-year-old (a rancher's term for two-years-plus). We brought him down and gelded (castrated) him and shortly after, started breaking him. He sure didn't like that.

I rode him working the ranch but had to buck him out every day—every morning I got on him he would buck. He was a good stock horse but he was mean. When working cattle, he could go all day where most horses would have to change two or three times. Yes—we sure had to watch or he would kick us or bite us, just anything to hurt us. Mom hated him.

One morning, I was trying to saddle him and he got me in a corner of the corral trying to paw me, and I heard a 30-30 being cocked. I saw Mom on the fence fixing to shoot Majesty. I talked her out of it. Daddy said, "We'll teach him better than that." So he fixed him in a team with Buck and Billy, a couple of our mules, and I got to plow the field and work on the flood tank. I worked them two or three months before I went into the service. I don't think they did much with him while I was gone.

When I got back, Daddy said, "It is time you do something with Majesty." Okay, we saddled him and snubbed him up to the saddle horn of Colonel (a big, strong, chestnut sorrel stallion) with Daddy in control, and I slipped onto Majesty. He acted like he had never been ridden. He bucked until he fell down, but I stayed with him and when he got up, Daddy turned him loose. I rode him over to *Black Rock Canyon* showing no mercy (about 9 or 10 miles).

I went back in the service shortly after that and told Daddy to do what he could with him. He traded him to a rodeo as a bucking horse—which he was good at for a while, but then he started slowing down. He was still mean, so they called Daddy to come get him. Daddy told Luther to take his saddle to school with him and bring Majesty home. So the school bus stopped at Mr. Watkins's garage and Luther left the saddle. The rodeo grounds were right across the highway. After school the bus let him off at the garage. When Luther showed up with his saddle the rodeo people just laughed at him. But Luther went in, saddled him and rode him home. Finally Daddy sold him for dog food.

So much for Majesty.

~ ~ ~

Luther, me and Billy Mule used a slip scraper to clean out the Cement Tank up on top of the mountain (I was about 15, Luther about 9). A slip scraper is a small 1-mule scoop as I described earlier.

The passageway in and out of the Cement Tank was very narrow and steep. After a few rounds to give Billy Mule the idea, we tied the reins up on the hames and Billy Mule got the message. Since I was a bit bigger than Luther, I worked down in the tank loading the scraper and Billy would take it up over the bank and Luther would unload.

Billy would come back for another load. I would stay down in the bottom of the tank and load the slip scraper and Billy Mule would take it up to the dirt dump. Luther would unload it and send Billy Mule back for another load.

I think Luther got the best of that deal. He sat up on top where there was a breeze. It was hot in the tank and Billy did most of the work.

~ ~ ~

We were all over at the Kretik's place branding their cattle. We had really been hard at it all morning. Luther and I were the cowboys. We did the gathering and what roping was necessary which wasn't much because the Orsak boys, Jody, Cyril, and Johnny, were tough as nails. They didn't tie a calf—they would just go in and grab a calf, three of them, and hold 'em down. They had never played football, and the first week out they were on first string—they were just that tough. They were pretty big guys.

We'd get the stock in the corral and they would go in and grab a calf and hold it while Daddy, Nadine, and a couple others would brand, crop the ears, castrate, and vaccinate. Mom would collect the mountain oysters (testicles) and fix them with biscuits and gravy to go with what the Kretiks fixed for lunch.

While we were taking a break for lunch, we got word of the attack on *Pearl Harbor*. I was 16 at the time and said I'd never get into it. It would be over before I got old enough to go.

Ida Jo Hass was there, but I guess I didn't pay much attention. When Luther and I got back to the ranch with the horses I was met by Mom and Daddy. They said, "Ralph, couldn't you see that Ida Jo was wanting to be with you? Why didn't you put her on Luther's horse and you two could have had some time together." Ida Jo was brought up a time or two later and I did have several dates with her, but I think that was about the time Jane Warren came into the picture.

Chapter 16
The Mule Skinner

Mules were equivalent to today's trucks. The dictionary says mule skinner is 'a driver of mules'. A mule skinner could drive a stage coach, a freight wagon, plow the fields—mules took the place of the trucks and the tractors. Anything a truck or tractor would be doing, the mules did. I say being a mule skinner is almost a lost skill.

A mule skinner is up at daylight or before and goes out to the corral and feeds grain to his mules. In order for each mule to get all of his grain we'd either use a nose bag—a bag you pull up over the mule's nose and tie a rope up over behind his ears and adjust it so when his grain is put in it he has a little space between his nose and the grain, so the boss mule can't take it away from him. Or—use a feed bucket and tie them off separate, so the boss mule can't take their grain away from them.

The grain is usually rolled oats or barley sprinkled with a little cottonseed meal. Daddy said that gives them a shiny coat. The mule skinner would then go in and have breakfast and get ready for the day.

This kind of work was hard on the hands, so Daddy would use goat tallow; put some salt in it and warm it just a little and we would rub it into our hands good. If our hands were rough and cracked, that salt sure did hurt. Daddy said, "That just makes them tough." Our left hand would get very heavily callused between the thumb and index finger and between the index finger and middle finger. It was difficult to wear gloves because that was our control finger and we needed the feel of the lines. We held both lines in our left hand with the index finger between them. Okay, the mule skinner was now ready to let his mules get a drink of water and start harnessing them.

Mules are very much individuals, each one has his own personality. Just like military GIs or teenagers.

After the mules had a chance to water, the mule skinner would go into the corral with a rope and some of the mules would let him just walk up and put the rope around its neck, but others he would have to lasso. He'd catch the mules one at a time and lead them out and harness them. He would put the blind bridle on so the mule couldn't see what the skinner was doing. Then he laid the collar pad over the mule's neck close to his shoulders. He would put the collar on over the pad and it buckled on the top.

The collars came in different sizes, so each mule would have his own collar. Then came the hames with the trace chains hung over them. They fit over the collar and buckled at the bottom. The trace chains hung down on each side between the hames and the back strap which would be positioned over the mule's back to keep the mule from getting tangled up in his own trace chains. They also sometimes used a belly band along with a back band. These were not cinched up tight, so that the mule had some space when the pulling got hard. The mule skinner would continue until all four mules were harnessed "four abreast".

They bring out a mule next to a fence and tie him to the fence or a rail to harness him—so they're side by side (abreast). Standing behind them, the mule on the right is number one and the mule on the left is number four—in front it would be like reading left to right … but they spend their time behind them, smelling them.

They're feeding them a lot of grain and they're passing a lot of wind, and it smells exactly like hardboiled eggs. Daddy used to say, "Any old mule can fart in the morning, but it takes a good mule to fart at night." Working all day they've used up all that, but only a strong mule could do it at night.

Harnessing took some time to get it just right.

We are now ready to head for the job site. When we were building *Basset Lake*, it was close. But later on it might be a quarter mile down there, and we didn't haul the Fresno and equipment back and forth ... it was left there at night. We could either walk and drive the team, or we could ride one of the mules and drive the team. We never knew how far away from the corrals the job site would be.

 If it is a dirt moving job, we must first decide if we'd have enough loose dirt to last till noon or should we first use the plow to loosen up some ground. Next we'd hook up to the plow or the Fresno and start our day.

If we were using the Fresno we'd have to plan our circles to move the most yardage of dirt with fewest number of circles and keeping our mules' welfare in mind. We were trying to take the dirt from one point to another point ... it makes a circle, because we had to come back to the same point and pick up more dirt. We'd plan so one load goes next to the last load, and the last load is the lightest, stacking one load on top of another load, just like working with a tractor today. We'd figure out how to get all the plowing or scraping done the easiest way. The manner in how we'd manage the dirt made all the difference. The man who can manage the dirt can get the job done in a whole lot less time.

An hour break at noon and then start all over again in the afternoon for another four hours. If the corrals were a long way off, we'd bring the grain and water to the mules for their noon break, but if the corrals are close we'd take the mules to the corrals for the noon break. We would switch back and forth with plow and Fresno (plow would loosen the dirt up so the Fresno could scrape it up) to keep the most dirt moving. The idea is to move as much dirt as possible in the least amount of time.

Daddy was very particular about his mules. He did NOT allow a skinner to curse or whip his mules. We handled them by talking to them, calling them by name and popping them with the lines (some people call them reins).

I would sometimes get so mad at a mule that I would curse them but always under my breath. If a mule didn't pull his share, or stop, or want to go back to the corral—and a mule can be stubborn—I'd get mad at 'em because he didn't do what he was supposed to be doing. But they would work better by talking to 'em and calling by name, and they knew their names, and slapping them with the reins— which didn't hurt them but they knew that I was there. I was handling this 4-mule team with my left hand because I was using my right arm in handling the equipment—the handle of the Fresno. I wouldn't put my thumb around it because if I hit a rock and couldn't get my thumb off of it, it would break it like a crank on a Model T. I didn't do a plow the same way at all. I'd tie the lines together and put them across my shoulders because I'd need both hands on the plow. So I was controlling the 4-mule team with my shoulders and both hands are on the plow.

The jobs I remember most are the *Bassett Lake* down by Montie's, the Railroad Spur at the fluorspar mill northwest of *Deming*, the Red Tank on top of the *Little Florida Mountain*s and of course we were always working on the flood tank above the ranch house.

The first two jobs, I was too young to be a mule skinner so I was the wrangler and took care of feeding and watering of the mules. On the Red Tank I did the planning, the layout, and was the number one mule skinner. You could say I built the Red Tank under Daddy's close supervision. He said that the new heavy modern equipment (bulldozers and tractors) was a passing thing and would NEVER replace the mule, so I needed to know how to work and take care of the mules. It seems strange that I was working part-time for Mark Terry as his grease monkey on heavy equipment building the highway into *Reserve, New Mexico*.

~ ~ ~

While working in *El Paso*, Daddy met the Wilhelm family. They were Seventh-day Adventists and got to be good friends. They had

A Cowboy Goes to War

several children. A son Dave was about a year older than myself. Daddy brought him up to the ranch one weekend and he stayed a couple of weeks with me. His dad worked on the railroad so he had a passenger pass if he needed it.

Daddy was telling stories how as a young man he had ridden the rails and dodged the railroad bulls (security guards to keep everybody off the trains, and they were usually mean). Up underneath the box car there were rods to brace the train up. Hobos would climb up on the tie rods underneath the boxcars so the bulls couldn't see them. They called this *riding the rails*. Daddy had gone to *Wyoming* to compete in a rodeo in *Cheyenne*. I didn't hear any more about the rodeo, only the trip. So I guess he didn't do so well. Anyway, Dave and I decided we wanted to try it, so Daddy said, "Only for the weekend, 'cause we have work to do." So we left on Friday and drove the Model T over and hid it in the brush east of *Deming* and caught a freight as it rolled out of *Deming* before it got up much speed.

It worked pretty well except it pulled onto a siding in *Akela* for a four-hour wait. Dave and I got thirsty and went over to the section foreman's to ask for a drink of water. There was a man, a woman, a young girl, and a younger boy. The man says, "Sure!" and turned on a hose. We got a drink and went on back to the train. *I didn't know it then, but the young girl became my wife and we raised five children.*

The train finally got rolling and we were playing tag on top of the cars. When we got close to *El Paso* and we looked up, we were coming to a tunnel. Golly we were scared! So we flattened out on top of that boxcar. Really we had plenty of room but by the time we got through that tunnel, we looked like we had come from much farther south. We nearly choked on that coal smoke and our complexions got much darker.

Not much happened in *El Paso*. We ate a lot and visited a lot and went to church on Saturday. We got up Sunday morning and headed back for the ranch. Our trip back was old hat now, uneventful till we picked up the Model T. We were going along on a winding two-track road and the Model T wasn't running very well, so Dave was sitting up on the right front fender messing with the coils. The road made a quick turn to the left but Dave didn't. He went sprawling out into the mesquite brush. When he got back into the Model T his right arm was really hurting.

We got to the ranch and Mom said, "That arm is broken." She wrapped it up pretty good and made him a sling. Mom took him back to *Deming* in time to catch the evening passenger train to *El Paso* using Dave's railroad pass. I didn't see Dave until the next year when school was out. He had graduated from high school and was going into the military. He wanted to come up and say goodbye.

He stayed about a week and we took the freight train back so I could spend the weekend with him before he had to go. Mom said, "We will take you over to catch the freight." Nadine said, "I am going too!" Mom and Daddy said, "Oh no, you are not!" Nadine said, "I could dress up like a boy and nobody could tell the difference." She sure did put up a good case, but she lost. Dave and I enjoyed our last trip and the week together, but Sunday we said our goodbyes and he went down with me to catch a freight train. It wasn't the same without Dave.

When I got a little west of *El Paso*, my train took the south track to *Columbus* rather than to *Deming*. I got off in *Columbus* and got a drink of water and a bottle of water and started up the highway toward *Deming*. I hadn't gotten more than two or three miles when a Model A coupe stopped and picked me up. The driver was a college student from *Las Cruces*. He and his friend were taking Geology and were interested in the *Little Florida Mountains*.

They came up to rent horses from Uncle Jim but when they got there they couldn't both afford it so they flipped a coin and his buddy got the horse. "Hey—if you will take me over to the ranch, we will saddle up the horses and show you that mountain." He did and we did. Nadine, Luther and I took him up over the *West Trail* by the

Coleman Hole, the May tank, to *Agate Peak* and back to the ranch by the way of the *Big Gap*. He had our saddle bags just full of rocks. We got to running and playing out on flat ground and the saddle bags tore open. He got down and saved most of them and just kept apologizing for ripping the bag. He said, "I'll send you a new one." Within a week we had a new one.

I never rode a freight train again.

Chapter 17
West Trail Dam

Daddy got approval on a government project to build a cement dam in the bluffs just above the *Coleman Hole*. Well, the cement and sand had to be packed up there. We packed enough cement, sand and water to build some little dams to catch water for the project, then the work started.

Luther and I would go over to the *Mimbres* riverbed with the Model T and get sand. We would take 10 tow sacks and Daddy wanted about 100 lbs. in each one. I was about 13 and didn't weigh but about 80 lbs., so we would put about 50 or 60 lbs. in a sack and drag it into the Model T, then shovel by shovel bring it up to Daddy's mark of 100 lbs. We would take it up high on the slope of the mountain, south of where Nadine's house is now, to the foot of the *West Trail*.

Loading the donkeys: when we got the sand and cement up to the foot of the *West Trail*, we needed to figure a way to pick up 200 lbs. and put it on the donkey's back. We set up a tripod with a block and tackle on it, and we could drag the bags out of the Model T over under the tripod, tie two of them together and pull them up in the air, lead a donkey under it and let it down. We did the same way with sacks of cement. Luther helped me with all of this but I can't remember him going on top with me. I can remember making two trips a day with five donkeys.

The tripod consisted of three long poles tied together at the top to look sorta like a teepee. We would tie a block and tackle in the top of it. We dragged the sand or cement over under the tripod and tied them together at the top so they could hang over the pack saddle on the donkey. That made each donkey carrying about 200 lbs. We would lift it up in the air with the block and tackle, high enough to lead a donkey under it, let it down across the pack saddle, and secure it. No, the donkeys didn't like it and I had to get their attention a time or two and convince them that they were not supposed to rub it off against a tree. Then we got along pretty good.

Up the trail we would go. After a few trips we would load Jenny first and she would start on up the trail. Jenny was our lead donkey. I was riding a horse named Smokey that wasn't liked because he had an iron jaw ... he'd grab the bit in his mouth and take off with us. Daddy fixed me a pretty good-sized stick I could hang on the saddle. He said, "When he starts that, use that stick and either cure him or kill him 'cause he is no good to us like that." You know, it didn't take us long to come to a good understanding.

Oh I made a bunch of trips up that *West Trail*. I am sure that all signs of the sand are gone, but I think you will still find several sacks of hardened cement on the upper side of the bluff above the *Coleman Hole* on the south side of the canyon. The project was never completed because the bluffs had too many cracks in them and we could never find a place that met government approval.

Chapter 18
Military Life— How It All Began

Early Military

While I was horseback riding on the *Little Floridas* (Spanish, *Flow-ree-dahs*) looking after the cattle, up by the Indian Post Office, I saw a T-11 training plane heading east out of *Deming*, and watched it drop a bomb almost overhead then saw it hit a target *way out* in the flats east of the *Floridas*.

Getting off my horse, I said a little prayer, "Dear Lord, if at all possible that's what I'd like to do."

I went home and told Mom about it, and she got ahold of Miss Whitehill, one of the high school teachers. I was a year behind in school, but she said that if I followed her instructions exactly, she could get me ready for the cadet program. A year later, I was enrolled in cadets and became a second lieutenant on September 2, 1944.

I needed more school credits so I could get my high school diploma and qualify for cadets. Miss Whitehill set up some things for extra credit. I wasn't the only one trying to do the same thing.

There was a government program for ranches that would furnish money for equipment and supplies for a project if the rancher would furnish the labor. Well, Daddy wanted to build the Red Tank up on the mountain.

Miss Whitehill arranged for me to draft the drawings, figure the yards of dirt to be moved, shape of the tank, the angle of the dam to hold the most water, and how much water it would hold. I had to figure the man hours, the mule team hours and cost of moving everything up there. There wasn't a road to the site yet so everything had to be packed in on mules.

We had to pack a Fresno on a mule, tearing it down to its smallest parts and putting it back together again when we got there; it was the same with the plow.

A Fresno is a metal scoop about four feet long, with a blade on the front of it and a skid on each end. In the back it had a long handle with a rope dragging from the end of it, and pulled by a four-mule team.

The driver handled the mule team with the left hand and the Fresno with the right hand. He'd lift up on the handle and the blade would cut into the dirt and would load the Fresno. When it got to where he wanted to dump it, he pulled up on the handle sharply and the blade would catch and dump the load—the handle would go straight up in the air. After dumping the load, it pulled real easy—grab the dangling rope, pull it back down to the loading area and reload it.

It was a very dangerous thing because if the blade hit a rock—and we were in rocky country—the handle would come up and take an arm off. So we worked with our arm as far out from our body as we could get it. Using a plow to loosen up the ground was just as dangerous—trying to hold the plow with both hands while handling the team with our shoulders (tie the lines together and put them around our shoulders). We were in rocks and the plow bounced and jumped—I was small and scrawny and weighed about 100 pounds.

I had to show how many Fresno loads per yards of dirt, and how many loads a team could haul per hour. We had to also consider the time to loosen the ground with a plow. The doing was a hell of a lot harder than the figuring.

Miss Whitehill set it up so I had to get up in front of all the math classes with a blackboard and explain how I came up with all this information. I did it and got extra credits for math and communication. They have served me well. By the way, after 70 years with a lot of hard knocks and bumps in the road, the Red Tank is still there.

United States Army Cadet Program

On June 21, 1943, I entered the service at age 18.

I flunked two semesters of grade school. They had grades 2A and 2B, and I flunked my whole second grade at seven years old. I decided to be a rancher like my daddy, and I didn't think I needed all that education to take care of cows. In the fifth grade I began to wake up, and by Junior High I was on the Honor Roll, but I was a year behind. Then I got into High School—16 years old. The draft would get me before I graduated, and that's when I ran off to *California*.

It was summertime and I was going to join the Navy. I was too young to join, and I found out Mom and Dad had me deferred from the draft because I was working on the ranch. So I came back to the ranch, then—that's when I was riding up on the mountain, got off my horse and prayed. I went back to high school (fall of 1942) a sophomore.

I never was a junior—only a freshman, sophomore, and senior. Miss Whitehill set me up on a rigid program to get the required credits to graduate from high school before I got drafted. By signing up to attempt to get into the Army Cadet program and excluding me from the draft until June 21, 1943, I had to volunteer to be drafted in order to overcome the deferment Mom and Dad had for me. I had done two years of high school work in one year.

I volunteered to be drafted and reported for duty on June 21st at *Sheppard Air Force Base* out of *Amarillo, Texas*. I went through 6 weeks of Army Basic Training. From there went to *Oklahoma* Women's Baptist University in *Shawnee, Oklahoma*. We spent ten weeks learning navigation, Morse code and math.

We were in a women's university, but were strictly quarantined to our quarters. Because we were there over Thanksgiving, we put our names on the board for someone to come and take us to dinner.

~ ~ ~

An Indian family invited me to Thanksgiving dinner. We went out to their rural place where they had horses and cattle. They figured I would be a dude like those they had had previously.

I told them, "Yeah, I can ride. I came from a ranch in *New Mexico.*"

So the girl about my age said, "Well, come with me."

When we got out to the corral, she threw me a bridle and she took a bridle and said, "You ride the paint." So I put the bridle on the paint, and she put her bridle on a little dun then jumped on him. That's when I realized we weren't gonna use saddles. We rode off down through the pasture and through the creek. I think she took me everywhere she thought I couldn't go. We had a good time riding then went back and had a nice dinner. I had a curfew so I had to get back to quarters.

~ ~ ~

Later, we were housed in an old drive-in hamburger joint and were called The 'Mc' Flight—some spelled Mc, some Mac, all of McDougal, McFadden and McCrary—26 of us, with a Michael and a Mitchell in with us. We finished our training there and went to *Ellington Air Force Base, Houston, Texas* for about six weeks, taking our preflight training (the academics of flight).

After about a month, we got our first weekend off and some of us went into *Houston* by cattle trucks set up with a rope strung up and we hung onto the rope.

At a USO there were quite a few girls, and I met Hilary Evans that Saturday evening. I came back Sunday morning and went to church with her then we went ice skating Sunday afternoon. I thought I was going to break both ankles!

From *Ellington* we went to *Laredo Air Force Base, Texas*, for gunnery training.

That was intensive training, firing the .30 caliber and .50 caliber machine guns. Because of my size, being so small, I specialized in the Sperry Ball Turret that hung down below the B-24s and B-17s.

One day they called us to a formation and gave the command, "Dress right dress!"

We all turned our heads right and lifted our left arms up 90 degrees and touched the man next to us.

The person in charge gave the order, "If you're taller than the man to your right, move up."

I kept moving right until a taller man stood on my right side. Then I did a right-face and did the same thing again. The tallest man ended up at the far right corner and the shortest man in the left back corner.

Then the man in charge walked through and chopped off the rear left corner for Sperry Ball.

A big person couldn't operate it. The gunner had to sit in an almost fetal position with a .50 caliber on each side and gun sight between them.

Two small handles controlled the weapon, with thumb triggers on the top of them. A sideward motion turned the guns for azimuth 360 degrees, and a fore and aft forward motion controlled the 90 degrees elevation.

I was never in combat with the Sperry.

Harry McCrary and I competed in the regular turret mounted on a 6 x 6 army truck and we ran a course with clay pigeons flying out from an unseen site. We had to get on them with our turrets and use our elevation and sights to shoot them down. We each had 100 rounds, and he beat me. He got 99/100 and I got 98, but he beat me and he let me know it.

At gunnery training in *Laredo*, we shot 100 rounds of ammo at a moving target. We had a big bank and a road on the other side of it. The target would run along behind the bank and we'd shoot at it.

One day, we sat ready at the machine guns when a hawk flew over. Two instructors pushed two guys aside, took over the machine guns and started firing at the hawk. They fired off at least 200 rounds of ammo and the hawk flew away.

Then we shipped out to *Webb Air Force Base* in *Big Springs, Texas*, for training in four categories, pilot, navigator, bombardier and bombardier/navigator. I went to the bulletin board to see what my destiny was and at first I was disappointed at not being a pilot. But then I thought about it. *Well ... I'm not just one, I'm two. Bombardier/Navigator.*

When I told Mom I planned to be a bombardier, she became upset about me killing all those people. I had planned to be a pilot, but during training I found that I didn't have good depth perception. Instead of washing me out, I became a bombardier instead of a pilot.

At *Webb Air Force Base*, three cadets would go out with an instructor pilot and copilot in an AT-11 (Advanced Trainer). One student would navigate, another bombs, the third would take pictures. Then we traded places and repeated the training exercise.

We were in tough competition and were graded by the *circular-error* to graduate. The target was called a *shack* with circles around it at given distances. Bomb strikes had to be within the circles and close to the shack to graduate. The further out the pattern of bomb strikes from the target, measured by the circles, were called *circular-error.*

In our area, local civilian oil wells were lit up at night similar to what the military practice target looked like. Some cadets were getting confused and bombed the oil wells. So, when we were scheduled to train in their area, the oil wells would turn off their lights. The bombs were sand-filled with a 5-lb smoke charge in the rear that went off so we could photograph it.

On one of our missions, we came in for a landing and had the flaps down. Just as we touched, the pilot called for "flaps up", and the copilot pulled the gear up instead of the flaps. We bellied in, tore up the bottom of the aircraft and ruined both engines. They sent the meat wagon out and we had to go to the flight surgeon to make sure we were okay. The AT-11s immediately got a safety feature installed so that couldn't happen again.

Another incident I was involved with was coming in from a mission running real low on fuel. There was a thunderstorm coming to the base and we were trying to get there before the thunderstorm hit. We got down on the runway all right and pulled off onto the ramp, but while sitting there running our engines and holding against the wind, a B-26 in maintenance blew loose and rolled into us, bending our left wing and ruining the left engine.

It was at *Webb Air Force Base, Big Springs, Texas*, that I graduated from Cadets and became a 2nd Lieutenant in the Army Air Corps. At this point, I gave up my enlisted serial number 38441334 and received an officer's serial number O-2070294. When I came back in as an enlisted man, I took the enlisted number again. Then when we changed from Army Air Corps to U.S. Air Force, my serial number changed to my Social Security number.

All this time as Cadets, we went through hazing, the cadre trying their best to wash us out. Of the people who started at *Ellington*, only 30% graduated. Those who washed out automatically became gunners because they were already trained, ready to go.

September 2, 1944

After graduation, we were sent home on two weeks leave. I had to go home and show off my big gold, second lieutenant bars. Then I had to report to *Shreveport, Louisiana, Barksdale Air Force Base*, OTU (Overseas Training Unit), and that was where I learned that I would be assigned for training as member of a B-26 crew.

Our requirement was to fly 120 hours, getting familiar with crew assignments, the aircraft and practicing our skills. We no longer had the hazing.

We were scheduled for two missions a day including day and night flights with two hours off on Sunday.

The B-26 soon acquired the reputation of the widow-maker and the saying, "One a day in *Tampa Bay*," by losing one airplane every day in training among all three Air Force Bases doing B-26 training.

One early morning, we sat on the ramp running up our engines before takeoff when the right propeller came off and started flopping down the ramp. That didn't give us much confidence in our plane.

Another incident happened when the boys got to feeding a dog at the mess hall. We went out, started up the engines and the dog came running to the plane. He ran into the propellers, and it just about made hamburger of him.

Chapter 19
Bombardier/Navigator

1943—1946: World War II

After OTU, I went overseas on the *Queen Elizabeth* with 22,000 troops and officers. That was important because it was fast and could outrun the German subs. We kept a zigzag course so if they tried to intercept us we'd change course and they couldn't predict where we'd be at a given time. It took us three and a half days.

My first assignment was Funeral Services Officer in *DeJong, France*. I didn't do much but just be there most of the time. The people we had services for weren't there because they had gone down and the bodies had not been recovered.

During the ceremony, taps would be played with echo from beyond the ridge. I was so impressed. I would bring the troops to attention, lower the flag and retire it. I was brand new and it was the only time I did this.

Normally, there are six men on a B-26 flight crew: Pilot and Copilot, Bombardier/Navigator, Engineer, Radio Operator, and Turret Gunner. On a group lead mission, the group lead plane carried eight people, the regular crew plus a photographer and mission commander. Our normal speed going into a target was 180 knots (207 miles per hour). Leaving a target was 210 knots (240 miles per hour) and always in formation.

Before starting the engines on a B-26, the prop had to be *run through*. Each man would grab a blade of the prop, put his shoulder against it and push it as far as he could. The next man would do the same thing, six men on each prop, so that it got one and a half revolutions on each prop. They did both props to clear the oil out of the bottom cylinders. If that wasn't done, the pistons could break.

A B-26 has two R2800 cubic inch engines made by Pratt & Whitney and created 2,000 horsepower apiece with a total of 4,000 horsepower.

The British flew their missions at night, and they never flew in formation, I never knew why. The U.S. always flew missions during the day and always in formation.

If one of our planes was shot down, another plane just moved right in and kept our formation. That's just the way we did it. We never crashed into each other while the planes were in formation.

While I was flying, I got airsick when it got rough, but it had to get pretty bad before I got sick. I always carried a bag with me, and I learned to vomit and go on through it. Then I began to watch my diet before flying and it did make a difference. I'd avoid greasy or spicy things. I never got sick during a combat run because we had to hold formation, which was a steadier flight, but it made me wonder if my problem wasn't psychological.

I was in the Army Air Corps from 1943 to 1947 then changed to United States Air Force in 1947. I received awards from both Army and Air Force during my twenty years in the Air Force and a little over three years while in the Army.

Chapter 20
Togglier & Big Red Team

On my first three missions, I was *togglier*, but I didn't use the device. Each plane had a bombardier/navigator in it, but only the lead plane actually used the Norden bombsight. When the person designated as the togglier saw the lead plane's bombs come out, he hit the toggle switch to drop his bombs. Therefore, he was known as a togglier rather than a bombardier.

Then they selected navigators.

I was in training and on our seventh mission with Captain Pierce flying in the number three position when the flight leader got shot down. We watched two chutes come out okay then saw a third chute come out burning. Five men still remained inside when the plane went in. The number two plane couldn't take the lead because his equipment was shot up too bad, so we went in the lead.

We got 100% mission on approach to the Heidelberg Bridge, but weren't allowed to hit the bridge. We were to ruin the approach so they couldn't use it.

Under adverse circumstances, we made 100% mission and received the air medal. After the mission, Captain Pierce requested me as his navigator and Joe Feller as his flight engineer. I have a directional sense that does not depend on visibility. If my instrument didn't work right, I could sense it, so I never got turned around in mountains.

Daddy was that way and he was a hunting guide in the *Gila* wilderness. I can't describe how this directional sense works, but I have a hunch it may be magnetic somehow.

A Cowboy Goes to War

I was a Group Lead Navigator with Capt. Pierce and Joe Feller, called the Big Red Team. Our airplane had a big red tail with a 29 on it. The secret is, I think I got to be Capt. Pierce's lead navigator because he got my double shot of bourbon when we landed.

I wasn't a teetotaller, but when we went out, I would order a *Cuba Libre* (rum and coke with a twist of lime) then drink them all night. After the first drink they were all virgin. When I got my first one, I would instruct the bartender that I was the ranking man so he was glad to take care of me. Later on, I made friends with him.

~ ~ ~

The men who had been in the unit the longest, traded soap, candy, and cigarettes—all good trading items. They also had someone lined up who would get their things if they were shot down.

When we got back from a mission, we were given medicinal liquor (a shot of bourbon) and a debriefing. We knew who was shot down, so after the shots of whiskey and debriefing, the next point was to divvy up stuff of the people who didn't come back. Whoever was to receive a guy's stuff got it. A person who was lost—we never spoke of him again. It was like he'd gone home.

As far as we were all concerned, it was a one-way mission, and we were being replaced all the time. We lost a lot of men, and we didn't really get scared till the last few missions. I always thought, *We might make it*.

In my crew, the oldest guy, Pappy, was 23 years old, so was my pilot Capt. Pierce. Our Commander, Col. Gray, was 26. The rest of us were all a bunch of kids. I was 19 when I went over in December and was 20 years old in February.

Our group, 320th Bomb Group, was in direct support of General Patton and the French Army. Our group consisted of four squadrons, with nine airplanes in each squadron. Each group consisted of 36 airplanes.

Ralph McDougal

Our sister group was the 319th Bomb Group. They also had 36 planes, so when we flew together, we had 72 planes. We flew flight squadron formation of nine planes.

The 8th Air Force flew a box formation of 12 airplanes per squadron. It is understood that there are more planes on the ground for each squadron that are in a state of maintenance or repair.

We went over as crews, six at a time. My crew consisted of pilot Guedel, copilot Bill Myers, me as bombardier/navigator, engineer Sergeant Joe Feller, radar man Isador Grady, gunner Sam Phaland. Bill Myers was taken out on the second mission. Isador Grady and Sam received flak in the midsection, were hospitalized and ready to go again, but they were replaced. I don't know about Grady. Joe Feller and I went with Captain Pierce and became the Big Red Team.

Ralph on R&R in London 1945.

At this time, I don't recall all the individual missions, just the ones where something special happened.

Squadrons were going out all the time (nine airplanes) but the Big Red Team only went on group missions made up of four squadrons, and sometimes two groups (72 planes). We didn't get as many missions as other guys because we were held back for group raids (36-72 planes) like on *Stuttgart, Heidelberg, Klein Engstingen, Po Valley* Raid and *Lahr Barracks*. The barracks were sitting there when we arrived, and when we left, there was nothing but a pile of trash. *Po Valley* raid, we strung them out. Flights of three planes, down in the valley on low altitude, taking out bridges and anything we could see that would take out the railroad because that was the supply line from the breadbasket in northern *Italy* to *Germany*, "feedin' 'em".

A Cowboy Goes to War

They shot at us from the peaks down into the canyon. We got hit pretty bad but didn't lose a plane. I can't remember, but in two missions we didn't get shot up. One was *Bordeaux Pocket* where we accidentally blew up the French Marines. It was interesting because we were up for the *Croix de guerre* (similar to a French *Flying Cross*, bright red with white tips, and lacy stuff on the cross). We saw one, but I never got to wear it. When we blew up the French Marines, they cancelled it.

When getting flak on a mission, I could feel almost everything that hit the plane. I felt kind of petrified, thinking, *What if the next one hits me?* But I didn't dwell on it because I had to concentrate on the mission. These things were just flashes.

We were on radio silence, meaning no one could use the radio over the air. We could use the intercom in the plane, but not the radio because the Germans could lock in on our radio signal and send fighters. It's just a knob turn on the intercom, is all.

I don't remember the mission target, but I kept track of any gun positions we encountered so we could dodge them on the way out. After completing the mission, we had to cross the autobahn (super-highway), and the Germans had moved two new gun positions in so we encountered them.

We were getting flak when one of our bombardiers, Lt. Beckman, hollered out, "I'm hit! I'm hit!"

He broke radio silence, but the pilot came back and said, "Where?"

Lt. Beckman said, "I dunno, but I'm hit."

So their plane broke formation and headed for home. They got to the base long before we did. When we got there, he came to meet us with a little sliver of aluminum in his hand. The flak had come through the aircraft and shaved off a little sliver of aluminum that stuck in Beckman's leg.

He was hollering, "Hey! I got a Purple Heart!"

Ralph McDougal

Of course, he was kidded for the rest of his time over there, but he got a Purple Heart all right.

~ ~ ~

There is one mission that I'm not very proud of. The 320th Group, 36 airplanes, was sent in on a fuel supply dump. We began getting flak as we went in.

When we saw fuel tanks the bombardier asked me, "Is that it?"

I said, "It looks like it to me."

So we bombed it. Two of the squadrons followed our lead and dropped their bombs, but the fourth squadron didn't drop. They went on in and hit the real fuel supply. What we hit were decoys.

Needless to say, that squadron all got air medals, but the other three didn't. The tanks sure looked real. They looked like big tanks with the pipes on them, but they were nothing more than mounds of dirt fixed up to look like tanks.

Fuel was one of Germany's biggest problems, and we were trying to get rid of it, of course.

The other time when we didn't get shot up, we were supporting General Patton, knocking out gun positions (with bombs) on the other side of the river in front of them so they could get across.

We went in behind his troops dropping the bombs over their heads and never got over enemy territory. That was really scary too, because just a little bit off and we'd have been knocking out ours.

About this time, the Germans came into the war with the ME 262 jets. We couldn't believe a plane could fly without a propeller, and we didn't know what to think. No propeller, how could it fly? And so fast. We didn't know anything about jets because to us, they hadn't been developed yet.

Those MEs could take off on the autobahn so we never could tell where they came from. They only had 12 minutes of fuel—the only thing that saved us, really—because we had no defense against them.

We had to change our way of using our turrets because they weren't fast enough to track, so we tried to aim our guns in such a way to make a wall of bullets for them to fly through. I don't know that we ever got one. We would lose three planes, at least, every time they hit us.

One mission, they hit the plane I was in and we had 11 machine gun bullet holes in our fuselage (thumb-sized holes clear through) from the rear edge of the left wing to the front edge of the right wing. A rocket went through the right wing between the rear edge of the wing and the tail end of the engine leaving a hole the size of a small washtub.

We got back okay.

They were after the lead aircraft (us) primarily, but we never even had to break formation.

On Easter Sunday 1945, we went after the ball bearing factory in *Stuttgart, Germany*, where they were making ball bearings for the ME 262 jets. The high altitude planes (B-17s and B-24s) which made several high-altitude raids, hadn't been successful. The 105mm antiaircraft guns were very successful at shooting them down. So they sent the B-26s (us) in at low altitude on a surprise attack.

The flak was so thick it looked like we could land on it, but they were having trouble getting our altitude. By the time they got it so they were hitting us, we had already dropped our bombs and headed for home, successfully wiping out the ball bearing factory.

Our plane had 142 flak holes and we had to break formation. We were on our own and our right engine was out. The right landing gear and tire were also out. We had no right windshield and it was colder than hell. Our stalling speed was 138 mph, and in our crippled condition, we were doing probably 145-150, just barely airborne.

We threw out everything that wasn't necessary to keep us in flight—everything but the Norden bombsight (it was classified secret, we had signed to protect it with our lives). We even threw out our flak suits (probably 35-40 lbs with the helmet). With eight people throwing them out, that amounted to over 300 lbs.

The lead plane carried eight people because it carried the commander and the photographer. That is when Sam and Grady got midsection wounds. We made it back sometime after the mission came in, but we were all alive. We were very fortunate that we didn't get hit by a German plane, because they were famous for shooting down wounded aircraft.

Bombing the ammunition dump at *Klein Engstingen*, we came over the mountains from west to east and we flew over a beautiful forest at about 8,000 feet. Ahead and below there was lots of farmland, divided by a road running north and south, with a little triangle forest running out into the farmland. That was our target.

I was group leader for 320th bomb group (36 planes). We hit first and circled back and the 319th bomb group (also 36 planes) mopped them up (dropped their bombs and finished the kill). They stayed in formation right behind us. Each one of the 72 planes carried 8,000 pounds of bombs, and we dumped the whole load, with 436 men, delivering 576,000 pounds of high explosives.

We didn't know what part of the forest area had the bombs in it, so we were instructed to take 72 planes (about the size of the forest area) and spread out to cover the whole forest at low altitude.

The bombardier/navigator had the highest mortality rate. By the time I got there, they had put armor plating for us to sit on up in the nose of the plane, and we wore flak suits. It was metal and heavy as hell. It was cloth with real flexible metal sewed into cloth. Two of us, the bombardier and the navigator, had to crawl into the nose, a space about 4 feet wide and 5 feet long.

The photograph below, taken by our plane's photographer, shows the plane behind us and smoke from our bombs as well as the ammunition dump exploding.

A Cowboy Goes to War

If you look close you can also see the little farms. Each mission had a mission commander, either a Major or Lt. Colonel, and he was in our lead plane, head of both groups.

We got an air medal on that one.

Ralph McDougal

The Norden bombsight, highly classified, I swore to protect it with my life. We'd sign it out each mission and were trained how to destroy it with a .45 caliber pistol. Each one of us in the crew had a .45.

In the B-26, the nose was glass or fiberglass. A rib goes down the middle and also around through the glass down to about halfway. Where the ribs came together is where a .50 caliber machine gun is mounted. It is hand operated and can be moved around. The gun sat above the Norden bombsight.

Behind the sight, there's a flat spot of armor plating that the bombardier would kneel on. The sight is down on the floor of the plane with the bombardier directly behind the bombsight.

There was a passageway into the nose and the copilot had to scoot over so we could get in. The bombardier was in the center. As the navigator, I would sit on the little step going into the nose and assist him.

It was my responsibility as navigator to get us to the IP (Initial Point) at the right altitude and the right heading. Speed is the pilot's responsibility, but at the IP we turned it over to the bombardier. He then controls the plane and the Norden bombsight until the drop.

After the drop, he turns it over to the pilot and I navigate the best route to get us out of there. I had all the charts and had already plotted the changes (gun positions) on the way in.

I'd look down and as we would see the flak positions—105mm is bigger flak than 88mm (bigger puffs of black smoke, bigger explosion) and got a bigger circle on my map. The 105s didn't move around as much as the 88s. These were antiaircraft guns—everybody in the plane would watch.

"Looks like there's an 88 out there."

I'd mark it.

Chapter 21
Intelligence Leak

Near the end of the war we had an intelligence leak.

After we got airborne and on our way to the target, Axis Sally would come on the radio and say, "Good morning, Big Red Team. We know you are coming and we know your target and we are ready for you. I would like to play some music for you on your way in. This is for Captain Pierce, Lieutenant Mac, and Sergeant Joe Feller."

Two songs I remember, *Symphony* and *Lili Marlene*.

It was scary that the Germans knew where we were going and what people were on the crew and could call us by name. It was scary as the dickens.

She didn't know, but we thought she did. After that we started briefing on three targets and we didn't know which one we would hit until *Roving Joe*, a Major on the front line, gave us the word.

To pre-brief a mission, we would start at about 2:00 in the morning and after getting the initial briefing, we would go to breakfast, then go back and brief the crews. The lead navigators would be briefing the navigators, pilots briefing the pilots, bombardiers the bombardiers and so on. Then we went out and ran the props through, normally a six-man crew; each man picking it up until we ran the props through several times.

After getting aboard, we started the engines then taxied and formed the group into 72 airplanes, preparing for take-off at five second intervals. Once in the air, we had to time our circles around the airfield so the planes taking off could join before heading out.

We had been at it for at least four hours. It was about 6:00 a.m. in the morning. The first planes would circle until the last plane could join them in formation then we were off on the mission.

Normally, the mission took four to five hours then we had to repeat the procedure for landing.

After landing, we got our double shot of medicinal bourbon. Then we went to debriefing. Intelligence wanted to find out what we saw on the mission, 105s or 88s, or fighters, gun positions, or a suspected new target. All were intelligence-type things they were gathering. All crews attended the first debriefing, because each man may have seen something different. Then the men were released, except for the lead pilots, navigators, and bombardiers for the second debriefing, just to discuss the mission for any improvements. We'd go to chow and by the time we got to chow, the rest of the group had already eaten and gone. We had mighty fine cooks.

This was a typical mission.

When we had to start briefing for three targets, it added 30-45 minutes to our pre-briefing.

The rest of it stayed the same.

We lined up for takeoff one morning, 72 planes (two groups) with a three-plane decoy taking off first. The construction people were putting lights on the runway and had about a two-foot ditch dug down the left side of the runway. The number three plane of the decoy blew a left tire and swerved to the left and ran his left landing gear into that ditch. By that time, he was doing well over 100 mph so it tore the gear off and collapsed the other gear. The plane was fully fueled with several hundred gallons of 100-octane gas, 8000 pounds of bombs, and thousands of rounds of .50 caliber ammo. Our plane was five seconds behind him with 71 planes following us.

When that plane caught on fire, we all chopped our engines, got out and ran like hell to hide behind the little piles of dirt the construction crew had piled along the runway. I went out the top hatch and ran right off the wing tip. One big drop.

Of course the gas created a very big fire. The .50-caliber rounds started popping off like fireworks, then the bombs blew. We had one big hole in the left side of the runway, but the first two decoy planes landed okay.

No one was hurt but our planes had some damage. The ground crew was great. They had the planes ready to make the mission the next day.

During one of our missions, 36 planes took off at five second intervals, climbed through an overcast and formed into units above the clouds then we headed for the target.

I was in the navigator's seat until we got pretty close to the target then I went up into the nose of the aircraft to assist the bombardier. After the drop and a lot of flak, I went back to the navigator's seat and—WOW—a piece of flak about the size of my thumb had come up through the bottom of the plane, up through my seat, and out the top of the plane.

That was too close.

Chapter 22
Victory in Europe

May 8, 1945: VE-Day

I was officer of the day. Every day there was a different officer in charge of the base on off-duty hours. When we got word that the war was over, everything exploded. Everyone went wild.

"The war is over! The war is over!"

I became busy with all kinds of things happening. People were on base that shouldn't be. It was a big responsibility.

Somebody shooting flares hit two of our planes.

Nothing was serious then, except the attitude of the French people because they immediately turned from friendly to, "GI go home. We don't need you anymore."

The guys who had women they were sleeping with, found they were no longer welcome. The women kicked them out and had nothing more to do with them.

A few days after VE-Day, Captain Pierce got word that his brother was being released from a prisoner of war camp at *Bari, Italy*. We got a plane ready and headed for *Bari*. We stopped for fuel by the *Leaning Tower of Pisa*.

When we got to *Bari*, they were working on the runway, so we had to land on the emergency strip. As we touched down, the left tire blew, so the pilot hit the right brake and that tire blew. The landing gear collapsed and we started spinning on our belly down the runway.

Six of us aboard and nobody hurt, but the plane was totaled.

We had Thanksgiving dinner aboard a navy ship. Oh boy, our first complete meal in over two years. It took about a week to get a plane in after us. Captain Pierce had a good visit with his brother.

After VE-Day, we would transport the enlisted men down to *Le Havre, France*, to be shipped home because they got to go home first. The runway was only 5,000 feet and minimum for a B-26 was 5,200 feet, but by dropping off our troops we could make airborne because there was a big, wide canyon off the end of the runway.

That big ole airplane had to rev up to 52 inches of mercury, release the brake, and off we'd go. We had to get up to 138 mph to take off. So we would go like a bat out of hell, and when we got to the end of the runway, we would pull up the landing gear and sail off into the canyon airborne.

We made several of those trips and did fine.

On one of the trips, we had been socked in for a couple of days and the troops' shipping date was getting very close. A hole opened up in the clouds and we figured we could get out above the clouds, so six planes took off and started up through the hole. We got up to 17,000 feet and our planes wouldn't go any higher and we still weren't above the clouds.

Four of the planes went back to base, but two of us went on IFR (instruments) and headed for *Le Havre*. We didn't get far into the clouds when we started icing up. We stalled out and started down and fell over 10,000 feet before we gained control of the plane.

Our troops had about decided they weren't going to get home after all, but we got them to the port on time.

After the war was over, we were sitting there with all these great planes and lots of fuel, so while waiting to be sent home, a lot of men that had been fighting on the ground had nothing to do. They had only seen the little area where they had been fighting. So we set up several planes to show them Europe.

Ralph McDougal

In Sint-Truiden, Belgium, holding a plane prop from a plane shot down.

The money exchange rate between each country was different so by planning it right, we could start out with $100, have a very good time (*France, Germany, Belgium, England*), and come back with more money than we started with.

We were limited to how much we could send home, but we sure had a good time while it lasted.

Married officers with kids or had combat longevity got to go home first with priority over Steve and me. We were assigned duties during the occupation of *Germany*. My duty was distributing new U.S. troops for the occupation. Steve was assigned as commander of the Polish army that had refused to go back home because of Russian occupation.

On one of my trips back from distributing the troops, I stopped by to visit Steve, a first lieutenant, responsible for a Polish general and his troops (three barracks) because they refused to go back to *Poland* and be put under Russian control.

Steve introduced me to the general, and the general asked us to wait just a few minutes and he left the room. He came back in about thirty minutes and asked us to go with him. He took us out to the first barrack (there were three two-story barracks) and as we would step into the door, for me to inspect the barracks, the troops would come to attention with the clicking of the heels, down one side and up the other side like dominoes. The footlockers were immaculate, and I was really impressed.

Steve just bought a new Leica camera (very popular, best you could buy back then). When we finished inspecting the third barracks, we came back to Steve's jeep and his camera was gone. The general asked us a few questions and told Steve he would take care of it.

I didn't see Steve for a coupla weeks, and when I did, I asked him, "Did you find out about your camera?"

He said, "Yes, but I wish I hadn't."

The general found the three men who stole the camera and they had traded the camera for a cow so that the outfit would have meat. The general called out the three men, pulled out his pistol and shot them on the spot.

Steve said, "I would gladly have traded the camera for a cow."

On another trip back from distributing the troops, I stopped in *Liege* (lee-aezh), *Belgium*, and checked into the BOQ (Bachelor Officers' Quarters) then went to the club and met a girl, Lou Rogin (roe-gun).

We danced quite a bit and between us, we drank a bottle of champagne. I spent about three nights before I went on. We drank champagne the first night, and then the second night I was still feeling the effects.

We did a lot of talking and a lot of dancing. She was very proper and on the third night, she took me up to meet her mother. Her father had been a doctor forced into service by the Germans and later killed.

During that time, we were stationed in *Sint-Truiden, Belgium* and were living in tents. While living in these tents, I pulled more KP as a lieutenant than ever before. Officers aren't supposed to pull KP, but the enlisted men had already gone home. There were three enlisted men and 360 officers. Enlisted men were the cooks and they really enjoyed bossing us officers around.

Sint-Truiden, Belgium, was pretty close to *Liege*, so I saw Lou on a pretty regular basis. That's when I went to see the chaplain and put in my paperwork to marry her.

The chaplain kept putting it off and putting it off then I was shipped to *Le Havre* to be transferred home. I went AWOL to see

Lou, and we discussed the thing and decided we'd let it ride to see what happened.

When I got back to *Le Havre*, they had marked my name off the list and was loading the ship, but I talked the sergeant-in-charge into putting me back on the list.

I sometimes wonder what would've happened if I'd been 10 minutes later. Life would have been different because I would have been court-martialed and given a dishonorable discharge.

I had several girlfriends overseas, but no one was like Lou. She was Jewish with a rather dark complexion and about as tall as I was.

Sometimes when I went on trips showing the guys Europe, we made money, and once I got her a pink cashmere sweater in *London*, something they couldn't get in *Belgium* at that time. That made a big hit. She was a very proper young lady, and I treated her that way.

The girl I went with most of the time over there was in *Dole, France*, Zhizelle Graviet (grav-ee-yae). At the time, we were housed in an old insane asylum. I dated her probably eight or nine months and was well accepted by her family.

Her dad was very strict and he locked big iron gates at a certain time every night, but Zhizelle climbed over. It wasn't the same feeling at all as Lou. We went to the club and all, but it wasn't the same.

I ate with the family on several occasions, and it was interesting. The meal was in courses. They always drank wine with their meals, and the children drank diluted wine.

Chapter 23
Buzzing—Low Altitude Flying

"You haven't lived until you've buzzed."

While flying about 50 feet above the ground over the rolling farmland of *France*, we came roaring over a hill and surprised a flock of pigeons that flew up and surprised us. One of the pigeons hit the front of the plane and put a hole in the glass where I was. I came back with pigeon guts and feathers all over me.

We had to explain why the pigeons were at 1500 feet.

Another time, we were in a three plane formation, flying over the North Sea and there was a mother ship with small fishing sailboats out around it.

Captain Pierce said to the other pilots, "Bet I can turn one of those over."

We circled around and came in about 25 feet off the water. Just as we got over a sailboat, we pulled up sharply and the prop wash blew the sailboat over. To prove it, we did it again, then the other two planes had to try their luck at it. They did do it, but ours was more precise. I've often wondered about the guys in the sailboat—were they okay? I wonder if they're still cussing us.

Another time, we buzzed a nudist colony. We didn't see anything, but nudes were running everywhere.

When we had nothing else to do, we would play tag when we were buzzing. We would touch each other. It was one of the dumbest things we ever did.

We'd be going to *Le Havre* in the B-26s and try to outrun each other. If we could outrun them, we'd come up and tap them on the wingtip with our wing. I wasn't afraid because we were playing. It wasn't a violent maneuver and we did it several times.

Ralph McDougal

Buzzing in jets is the height of life. We were right down on the ground. Three miles was no greater than three seconds with the adrenaline pumping. When buzzing, I'd have the same feeling as the takeoff at 640 knots (736 mph), just shy of the speed of sound. I'd go just above the telephone poles. The speed of sound is 740-752 miles per hour at sea level, normal weather conditions.

I never did go through the sound barrier. They said the plane (RB-57, reconnaissance version of the B-57) wasn't made to withstand it, but at 736 mph, I couldn't hear the huge jet engines inside the plane. I could just talk normally with no other sound. It was said we couldn't roll it, but we did.

Over *Europe*, we buzzed the B-26 at 210 knots, and I had to look awfully quick because everything was gone so fast.

In *Florida*, we'd see how close we could fly helicopters to an alligator before it jumped into the water.

We did have a lot of fun. We had the freedom to do it. Later they redlined it at 250 knots, but as far as Colonel Walsh and I were concerned, they ruined it.

After the war was over, I guess we were having too good a time with our planes, it was decided by someone that the B-26s were too hot and too dangerous for civilian use and had to be destroyed. Of course that really broke our hearts. So we flew them down to *Fürstenfeldbruck Air Base* near *Munich, Germany*, to be salvaged.

I understand that three of the B-26s escaped the ax. One of them is being restored at the *Pima Air and Space Museum* in *Tucson, Arizona*.

It is worth going to see.

I had my twenty-first birthday coming back from overseas on the ship *Laconia Victory*—a "victory ship". We got into an ice storm in the *North Atlantic*, and at the time, I was Garbage Control Officer. The ship iced up three inches all over the deck. I told the Navy that I couldn't put my people out there without safety factors. They brought out ropes and put them along by the rail so they could dump the garbage over the fantail—the back of the ship.

What I remember the most about the sea is it wasn't frozen over, but was broken ice. We were going slowly because of all the floating ice, and when we'd run into one of those pieces, it sounded like a can opener coming down the side of the ship. We expected at any moment for it to come through.

Laconia Victory was a tiny ship with around 200 of us on it, and while in that storm, I had my birthday.

In contrast, I went over on *Queen Elizabeth* (in 1944), 22,000 troops aboard. The war was already decided by the time I got there, and the end was in sight. But we didn't know that at the time.

Chapter 24
United States Air Force

When I was working so hard to get through high school, I only had one study hall. I always sat way in the back and there was a cute little girl that sat up near the front, and I could feel her looking at me. After a few days, I stared back. She smiled and I winked at her.

Boy that was a powerful wink because it took us through forty-nine and a half years of marriage.

At the time, I was president of the Future Farmers of America (FFA) and we sponsored a Donkey Baseball Game. Jane and I ditched school to gather up the donkeys and of course we had to take them home after the game was over. We had been on several dates together, but I had never kissed her and after gathering the donkeys, I took her by her house.

I kissed her goodnight and that went over so good I kissed her again. In later years, Mawmaw told me she opened the door and looked out and saw us then closed the door real quietly because she decided I was her future son-in-law.

We had that whole year in school together. Jane was eighth grade and about twelve or thirteen. I was sixteen or seventeen. We also put on a Banquet & Dance of which Jane was the belle of the ball. I got teased for robbing the cradle, but she was sure beautiful and had a nice shape.

Jane told me she had seen me before, but I didn't remember it. She said she would tell me some day. She told her friend that she was going to marry a little cowboy someday. So I felt that I didn't stand a chance.

A Cowboy Goes to War

I didn't see Jane very much the next year since she moved to *Lordsburg* (60 miles from *Deming*), but we kept in touch with letters and cards every two weeks or so. The mail was slow, and my mom and dad sometimes didn't go the ten miles into town to pick up our mail at the post office for several days.

When I got out of Cadets, I saw her while on leave before going overseas, and she wrote to me every day while I was in *Europe*.

Sometimes we wouldn't get mail for over a month at a time and my letters would consist of a big part of mail call. A lot of it was V-mail—Victory mail.

The military would take our letters and shoot a picture of them on 35mm film and then send it to be printed in very small print. During that time as an officer, part of my duties was to censor mail going home. All of us had a turn at it, just like doing KP. We even censored each other's mail. Anything that would reveal where we were or what we were doing would be blacked out.

~ ~ ~

When I came home from overseas, I went to *Summit* to see Jane several times between the last of February and the middle of April when she was a high school junior.

On my first visit to see her, I went to the school to pick her up. It was the last period and she was playing baseball.

Someone recognized me in my uniform and everybody hollered, "Here's Jane's Lieutenant!"

Jane interrupted the ballgame by running and hugging me. They insisted I come in and go up to bat. I dreaded it because I wasn't a good ball player, and I knocked three fouls in a row, way out there over their infield. Then I hit a home run and I bowed out while I was still ahead, all while in my uniform.

On the eighteenth of April, I finished up working on the windmill about 9:00 a.m. then went into the house and told Mom, "I'm getting married."

Ralph McDougal

She asked, "When?"

"Today."

"Have you asked her?"

"No ... not really."

"Have you asked her parents' consent?"

I answered, "No."

Mom asked, "Well, what are your plans?"

"I want you and Daddy to go with me. I am going to borrow Uncle Jack and Aunt Sue's car then drive over to *Summit* to get Jane's mom and come back to *Lordsburg* to get the license ... and go back to *Summit* and pick up Jane and her dad ... and her little brother and come back to *Lordsburg* and get married."

Mom asked, "Do you have a preacher lined up?"

I answered, "No, I don't."

We got ready and went to Aunt Sue's. Mom and Aunt Sue called *Lordsburg* and got a preacher lined up. We got to *Summit* and picked up Jane's mom and headed back for *Lordsburg* and met the school bus bringing Jane home. We stopped the bus and Jane got off.

We headed on into *Lordsburg* and Jane asked, "Where are we going?"

I said, "We are going to get a marriage license so we can get married this evening."

Jane said, "Oh ... well, okay."

We got the license and made arrangements with Reverend Foleoso to marry us that evening. Our next step was to go tell her dad and little brother Billy. That all went well, so we went back to *Lordsburg* and got married, April 18, 1946.

I was 21 in February and she would be 17 in May.

Just after we got married.

We went back to the ranch that night then up to *Black Range* to spend our three-day honeymoon camping. I found out she knew nothing about cooking, and she had never camped out. It started raining so we spent the next two nights in a motel.

We rented a little house in *Lordsburg* and I worked there for a while so Jane could finish her junior year of high school. Then I started college at *Socorro School of Mines*.

Alda signed me up, and she must have thought I was smart because she signed me up with classes way over my head. Plus the fact that after Cadets and combat, I just couldn't settle down. So Jane and I decided to try the service for a 4-year hitch.

After combat, we were riffed out of the Army because we weren't needed anymore, but we had a choice to come back in at the top enlisted rank, and that is what I did. I reenlisted as a master sergeant.

They called us *retreads*.

The hitch turned out to be a career of twenty-three years, three months, and two days.

~ ~ ~

My first assignment was in *Albuquerque, New Mexico* at *Kirtland Air Force Base*, while waiting for Aerial Photo School at *Lowry Army Air Corps Base* in *Denver*.

At *Denver*, we found a third story attic apartment on Adams Street by the City Park. We had a coal heater and the coal was in the basement. I had to carry the coal from the basement to the third story, and it was cold.

Ralph McDougal

On November the second, we had a twenty-four inch snowfall, so I had a three day school break. We spent a lot of time while we were in *Denver* at the City Park and at the *Museum of Natural History*.

Dwayne was born at *Fitzsimmons Military Hospital* on April 4, 1947. When Dwayne was very young, we moved back to *Albuquerque*.

We lived in *Belen* for a short while, then bought a little house in lower *Albuquerque*. That didn't last long because I got orders for *Japan*.

Chapter 25
Mapping the Empire of Japan

1947—1948: Reconnaissance in *Korea*

While stationed at *Yokota Air Base* in *Japan*, we flew three types of planes: F-9, a converted B-29; an F-7, a converted B-17; and an F-2, a converted C-45 (this basic plane was used in many configurations by all branches of the military) and many types of training planes: a twin-engine C-45 could be converted to an AT-11, AT-7 and many others to include the F-2.

During the time that we were photographing *Japan*, the North Korean military started building up, so we were sent on reconnaissance missions to fly the 38th parallel with large telephoto cameras which could reach approximately ten miles into *North Korea* to detect their military buildup.

We didn't fly over *North Korea*, but would fly those missions five to six days apart to detect if the buildup had changed from one mission to the next. On these missions, since I had been a navigator, I was navigating and had another photographer back on the cameras.

When we would come up to the 38th parallel, a North Korean MIG fighter would approach on the other side of the 38th parallel and he would fly with us across *Korea*, one of us on each side of the 38th parallel.

He was close enough that we could see him very plain.

When we got ready to go back, we'd wave at each other and each go our own way. I was very careful not to get over the line.

I could tell the area because it was a demilitarized zone—within about 100 yards. I don't remember how many missions we flew, but we did several of them.

We never did know how successful the pictures were, because as soon as we snapped them they became classified, so we took the film back and they were processed. We were never told the outcome of it.

Legally, I cannot say that I am a Korean veteran, because it didn't coincide with the beginning and ending dates of the Korean Conflict. I was only there for the buildup.

We mapped *Japan* for approximately one year, creating 20 feet x 30 feet mosaics of *Japan*. A mosaic is all the pictures put together to make a photograph of the entire *Empire of Japan*. We had a huge room which used to be a parachute rigging room where we laid out our mosaics.

A mosaic is made by taking an initial photo, then taking a matching photo that is 40% coverage of the initial photo and feather-edge it by taking a razor blade and cutting the emulsion (which is on the photo or slick side of the paper). Next, bend back the part not used, tear it off—thinner and thinner—and glue down the feathered edge.

Starting with one photo in the center, add them all around so the mosaic gets bigger and bigger. If one has a cloud, then we waited until we got one that didn't have a cloud and go back later and put it in.

We always had to make sure they were taken at the same altitude from about 9:00 a.m to 3:00 p.m. so it was well lit.

Many of the peaks of *Japan* were covered with clouds a big part of the time. We had to wait until the weather was right to get a clear picture, and boy when it was clear we would head for it, but many times, by the time we got there the weather wasn't right. We had to have a clear picture to tie the mosaic together. A 3-D scope on a little wire frame helped us line the pictures up correctly.

We could fly anytime, but whenever we flew, we had to spend eight hours in the air and use up the gas in the plane to keep getting our gas supply.

Beginning at *Chitose Air Base* on *Hokkaido, Japan*, the northernmost island, we were flying out of there, mapping, and

A Cowboy Goes to War

headed back south to *Yokota Air Base* on *Honshu Island*. It's like *Alaska*, so far north. While flying an F-2 back to *Yokota*, we looked out the right window and there was a huge volcano, kind of like *Mount St. Helens* looked after it erupted in 1980.

The pilot asked, "Do you think we could fly in that?"

"Let's try it," replied the copilot.

So we just stood on our left wing and did a 360 inside the cone. We flew a complete circle around the interior and back out to our flight path.

The lava was boiling down in the bottom. The sulfur smell was so strong, it would almost gag us. There was a bunch of volcanoes there, and it wasn't unusual to have several rumbles a day with earthquakes, and volcanoes erupting.

Most of *Japan* is that way, but *Hokkaido* is more so than the others.

On another trip, but in an F-7, we flew over the water between *Hokkaido* and *Honshu*, and a typhoon water spout spiraled up from the ocean as clouds spiraled down to meet it.

We decided to see what it was like to fly through it. It was rough as the dickens going in, and very, very calm for just a little bit. Then it got rough going out.

~ ~ ~

I went to Tokyo and everyone was talking about rickshaws. Opting for a ride, the driver was a little old man running down the street while pulling me. In my 20s, it embarrassed me to have an old man pulling me. Humbled, I paid him, got out and walked.

~ ~ ~

Ralph McDougal

I didn't fraternize with the people in *Japan*. I figured my wife would be just as true to me as I was to her, and she was. Most of the time, about 75-80% of the men just went and had a good time, but a few of us didn't.

~ ~ ~

About the time I got to *Japan*, we found out Jane was pregnant. Jane developed albumen poisoning and Dr. Watts of *Silver City* applied to Senator Chavez and got me home shortly after Darrell was born. Darrell was born in the car between *Summit* and *Lordsburg* when Pawpaw hit *Nine-Mile* dip. After he hit the dip, the back seat came out with Jane on it and Darrell crying.

I was on my way from *Japan*.

She was supposed to go to Dr. Watts in *Silver City*, but Pawpaw turned in to *Lordsburg* and the hospital wasn't going to accept her.

Pawpaw said, "You'll take her, or I'll tear this place apart!"

About six feet tall, Pawpaw weighed about 200 pounds. There was only a nurse on duty, and I guess she believed he would do it, so she took Jane in and cut the umbilical cord then cleaned her and Darrell up. By this time, the doctor got there and checked her out and they went on to *Silver City*.

Darrell was born with long red hair. They had already cut his hair by the time I saw him. This all happened on April 1, 1948. Yes, it was April Fools' Day.

I had a 30-day leave and was supposed to go back to *Japan*, but Dr. Watts didn't think I should, so with Senator Chavez they started the paperwork. Mawmaw kept Dwayne and Darrell while Jane and I went to *Travis Air Force Base* in *San Francisco* to await my orders.

Chapter 26
Berlin Airlift

1949—1951: *Biggs Air Force Base - El Paso, Texas*

The orders finally came and I was stationed at *Biggs Air Force Base* in *El Paso*, *Texas* in charge of the photo lab. We found a makeshift trailer on Truman St. for a while. During our stay there, Jane got real sunburned and the big birthmark on her back got infected. She got 138 penicillin shots to no avail, so they took it off. It left a 14-inch scar between her shoulder blades shaped like a carpenter's square.

After a few weeks, we rented a house on the *Tegua Indian Reservation* east of *El Paso*, but it was a long way to drive. I was one of three master sergeants (MSG) placed in charge of the Air Police.

Because I was working all hours, we let the house go and bought a 23-foot travel trailer. I built two small beds for Dwayne and Darrell above our bed then we moved onto the base.

This was during the *Berlin Airlift* and my hours were terrible, plus we discovered Jane was pregnant again. This was when the GI Bill was going well, so I got a GI loan and bought a neat new two-bedroom house.

We watched it being built. I paid $4,900 at 4% interest with $400 down. By the way, it is still a cute little house.

~ ~ ~

Debbie was born at the old *William Beaumont General Hospital* in *El Paso* on 25 May 1950. I got in some big trouble because that was before they let fathers in the labor room. They ran me out, but I would sneak back in.

About the third time they called the MPs and took me down to the guardhouse and I knew the sergeant on duty because I held the same position that he had, only over on *Biggs Air Force Base*.

I walked in and we greeted each other. He told his MPs, "I'll take it from here."

They left and so did I. I went back up to the labor room. The nurses had left to take Jane into the delivery room and Debbie was born on the gurney while on the way. The nurses just cut the umbilical cord then cleaned her up, and I had my beautiful girl.

During this time, we had a chance to spend a lot of time with my family at the ranch near *Deming*, and also with Jane's parents at *Akela*.

~ ~ ~

I'd been assigned to the Military Police during the *Berlin Airlift*, and was teaching my air police how to properly come to attention and salute when an officer approached the main gate.

During this training session, General Curtis LeMay, a four-star general and commander of SAC (Strategic Air Command), approached the gate with a security car ahead of him and behind him. I pushed the air police aside and told them I would demonstrate.

It had just rained and the ground was frozen and icy. When I snapped-to and clicked my heels, the motion knocked my feet out from under me and I fell flat on the ground beside the general's car.

To put it in perspective, being in charge of the air police, I was in Class A uniform, wore white leggings, a Sam Brown belt with a .45 caliber pistol on the right and ammunition on the left. I wore wings and ribbons and had an honor lanyard, a square-braided white cord which hung over my right shoulder with a whistle on it.

Imagine all that with me inside of it, lying beside the general's car. Now THAT was embarrassing.

I never lived that episode down until I headed for *Newfoundland*. It embarrasses me still to think that I did something that stupid.

A Cowboy Goes to War

~ ~ ~

After the *Berlin* Air Crisis was over, I went back to the photo lab during the *Cold War*. The policy of the U.S. at that time was to keep several B-29s in the air loaded with the proper munitions so they could counterstrike in case of an attack. My job was to copy the flight plans and put them in sealed envelopes that each crew carried and to be opened only in case of an attack.

All crews didn't get the same plan, and there were different plans for different areas. I was monitored by an Intelligence Officer who came to the lab when I had it all done, and he made sure that the right packages went to the right crews then we sealed them.

With the air police guarding outside I would stay in the lab at night by myself while I made copies of the plans for each aircraft that would fly out of *Biggs* on any given mission. The plans were already made up and because we didn't have copy machines, I copied them by camera.

I had to set up my lights, photograph the plans, process the film, and then print them.

It was all top secret.

Chapter 27
Newfoundland, Canada

1951—1953: Northeast Air Command - Photographic Advisor to the General Staff

In 1951, I got orders for *Newfoundland*, so we sold our house and rented a house for a month. While I went to *Newfoundland, Canada*, Jane and the children moved up to *Akela, New Mexico*. Pawpaw really threw a fit and wasn't going to let me take his daughter and grandchildren up there to live in igloos.

It took me about two weeks to find a place to live, a third floor apartment on Gower Street in downtown *St. John's, Newfoundland*. It was owned by an older couple that raised a family of nine children, two girls and seven boys. Most of the children were grown and out of the house, but still lived in or around *St. John's*.

The houses were built to look like a block-long house. Although they touched, each house was painted a different color with shutters in contrasting colors—dark blue with light blue, green with white, etc. They had all different colors and they were gorgeous and looked like something out of a storybook. Some were two stories and some four stories, so the roofline was very jagged. In many of them, the ground floor was a shop of some kind, boutiques and other little shops.

I got a 14-day leave to *New Mexico* to get the family, so I hitchhiked by military air. I went to the operations room and anything going west with space available, I took. On the second evening, I was at *Kirtland Air Force Base*, in *Albuquerque, New Mexico*, with little chance of finding anything going south, so I hit the road with my thumb. I made it to *Deming* in about 3 rides, with only one that I remember very well.

A Cowboy Goes to War

I had saved up $400 to come back on, and had it pinned to my undershirt. The first vehicle to stop was a pickup with two very drunk Mexicans in it. I was in uniform and they wanted to buy me a drink. I told them I was in a hurry to get back to my family.

Finally they gave up and one said, "You wait for us and we will get a drink … and then we will take you on with us."

As soon as they got out of sight, I took off running down the highway and caught a ride pretty quick. I never saw my Mexican friends again.

When I got to *Akela*, we had a lot to do to get ready for that kind of trip. We called *North Sydney, Nova Scotia*, and made reservations on the ferry, then by train for our 1946 Dodge sedan, luggage, trailer, myself, Jane, Dwayne, Darrell, and Debbie.

Of course we visited the family then started getting ready, trying to get everything we would need for two years. We loaded the car and trailer to the hilt then headed out. We had to make the reservation date to meet the ferry, and by the time we pulled out, I had only 5 days left.

The trip went fine and we made it with less than an hour to spare to meet our reservation time to board.

~ ~ ~

I had two jobs. One was building *Thule Air Base* which was called Project Blue Jay. I did the photo progress reports on building *Thule* (Too lee).

The other project was to make mosaics of the proposed detection and early warning sites in the artic.

Ralph McDougal

My Most Scary Experience

From *Newfoundland*, I flew over 2,000 miles to *Thule, Greenland*, and from Thule to a point on the northeast tip of *Greenland*, where they were talking about putting up a site for the detection and early warning system, somewhere about 1,000 miles from *Thule*.

We were over ice from *Thule* on, and all we could see was ice, no habitation at all. When we got to where we were supposed to be, the only way we could tell where land ended and the ocean began was by the ice cliffs being a different elevation from land and sea.

The compass didn't work because we were so close to the magnetic north pole, it just turned round and round. So we used a gyro compass and had to cage it every four hours and reset it so it would give us our directions.

All we could see was white. We had to fly out over the frozen ocean, come back over the ice bluffs toward the west, and take pictures of the proposed early warning site runway called *Nord*.

They needed maps of it, so I took the pictures to make the mosaic.

From there we headed to *Alert*, about 600 miles to the west. We flew one pass over *Alert* to take progress pictures for our Intelligence people. We came from there to T3, *Ice Island*, between the northern tip of *Greenland* and the *North Pole* (less than 100 miles from the *North Pole*).

I took photos of that setup for an alert site, then down to *Eureka*, nearly halfway to *Alaska*.

We came in on our pass and as we headed out of the little valley the number four engine (B-17) started acting up. So the pilot feathered it, but by the time we got it feathered, the vibration had shaken us up real bad.

Shortly after that, the number three engine went out, both out on the right side.

We had trouble holding altitude, but looking down below we were over broken sea ice, and the estimated time of survival is fifteen seconds. We were so far out we had no radio communication.

By trimming up and fighting the controls, the pilots kept it going. We were trying to reach *Greenland* so we could belly land on the ice cap.

It took us a long time and the pilots decided we'd have to land on the beach, but when we got there, we still had enough altitude to go above the cap, another 300 miles from *Thule*.

We headed south and finally came into radio range from *Thule*, and they reported a whiteout. That's when ice comes in like fog and we can't see anything. They can't send anything out and supposedly we couldn't go in, so we kept heading towards *Thule*.

I was more scared there than I was in combat.

When we got a little closer to *Thule* I could see *Mt. Dundas* sticking up above the ice fog, and I knew exactly its position in regard to *Thule*.

We flew west of *Dundas*, and although we couldn't do much maneuvering because we'd lose lift with no engines on the right, I lined up *Mt. Dundas* where I thought the runway was according to our instruments.

The pilot headed down into the ice fog and let his wheels down. We landed about 150 yards off the runway, but with everything being frozen, we landed okay.

A rough landing, but we landed safely, and of course, we were tickled to death to be on the ground.

We had been in the air 23 hours in a B-17 modified with fuel tanks in the bomb bay, two pilots, two copilots, an engineer, and myself. I acted as the navigator as well as the photographer.

Also, Maurice Mousset, who worked in the photo lab with me, went along for the ride. This was 1952, and I think that was the most scared I have ever been.

After taking pictures at *Nord*, we got the mosaics all made and it was decided where the runway was to be built. A B-17 was set with skis on it and a D8 CAT bulldozer was put in the belly of a C-119.

We escorted them into Nord with enough survival gear so the construction crew would be okay until we could get them out. Before the C-119 landed, they started the CAT.

The airplane landed on soft, powdery snow on top of the cap. They drove the bulldozer out of the plane and scraped off a runway for the C-119 to take off on. All the while on the ground, the C-119 pilot had to keep his engines running to keep them from freezing up.

All this time, we flew around in circles while taking pictures of them building a runway. We all got back to *Thule* without a serious incident.

Chapter 28
Aerial Photographer

1953–1957: 3206 Photo Test Wing - *Eglin Air Force Base, Florida*

My next assignment was *Eglin Air Force Base, Florida*. I had a 30-day leave that was spent in *New Mexico.*

Dot Soper from *Newfoundland* came down to join us and to move to *Florida* with us. I think she wanted to come to the states to find a husband, and she did.

I had rank enough that quarters were ready for us by the time our leave was up, and we lived on base for about a year and enjoyed it.

One day, I traded some stuff for an old fishing boat made out of cypress wood, about 15 feet long with a wide beam and flat bottom. It had a good sized deck and storage area underneath it. The engine was a one-lunger, one cylinder with an open-rod bearing and two big flywheels. Almost the same as the pump-jack engine we had at the ranch. We sure had fun with it.

Behind *Destin Beach* was a nice little shallow bay that we used a lot. We could gather shrimp, oysters and blue crabs. We got a regular yard rake and tied a bicycle basket onto it and would putt along real slow and rake up oysters off the bottom. I don't know of anybody else that did it, but it worked.

The propeller had a habit of coming off, but in that clear, shallow water we would find it and go under and put it back on. It got to leaking, and some of the locals told me to dry dock it and let it dry for a couple of weeks and the wood would shrink and leave some pretty big cracks. If we would pack the cracks with kapok and paint it with a special chemical paint and put it back in the water, the wood would swell again and seal it and the paint would protect it from the destructive bugs.

It worked.

We had to modify a little trailer we brought from the ranch to haul it on, and we really had fun. We never did learn to care much for oysters and we didn't catch many shrimp, but we took and ate our share of crabs.

~ ~ ~

I was NCOIC (Noncommissioned Officer in Charge) supervisor of the aerial photo department. During that time, I was Photo Test Chief on many new airplanes, the RB-57, B-52, F-84, F-101 and the B-66.

There were other types of aircraft that came through which I assigned aerial photographer chiefs to. The new planes came in fast and furious, and early jets were just coming into the inventory.

We tested each plane to evaluate and confirm their limits and capabilities.

When a manufacturing company would come in with an airplane, they'd say it could do this-this-and-this then we would test it to see if it could do what the manufacturer claimed it could do.

Often during the testing time, representatives from the manufacturing company would join us and in many cases when a problem would come up, and the plane could not perform as claimed, we would halt the project until the company corrected the problem, if possible.

Part of our job was to determine if the aircraft was practical. For example, I was photo test chief on the B-52, and it took 254 man-hours of maintenance on the airplane for every hour the airplane flew. Our job was to attempt to make it more practical by decreasing the man-hours of maintenance per hour of flight.

I didn't correct the procedure, I just recorded through photography whether it would perform the mission or not. Then I would use my photography to show whether they had a solution to the problem. This was before computers and modern technology.

Boeing came out with the B-52 and offered a choice of two interchangeable bomb bay capsules. The choice was munitions (military weapons) or reconnaissance (spying).

It wasn't so bad when the reconnaissance capsule was in there, because we didn't open the bomb bay. But when the munitions capsule was aboard, we had a problem with the electronics information being transferred from the aircraft to the rotating bomb bay. We had to prove that it would work. It did, but we did have some difficulties.

The chase plane was used to determine capabilities or problems that develop in the test airplane.

One good example, the B-52 developed metal fatigue in the fuselage that was caused by the difference in oscillating frequencies of the wing and the tail of the fuselage. It was causing metal fatigue on the fuselage, and the fuselage metal was deteriorating. We went up and took pictures that encompassed both wingtip and tail so we could determine the frequencies of each.

I don't know what they did to fix it, I just know that they did because there are B-52s still flying.

My job was to photograph the wingtip and tail from different positions. I was photographing from a T-33, a small two-man jet trainer, and in constant communication with the pilot to be in the right position to accomplish my mission.

The pilot of the B-52 said, "Okay, your time is up, we have to go on our mission."

He headed up and smoke rings came out of the eight engines.

My pilot said, "Well, let's just stay with him awhile."

The B-52 flat ran off and left us.

The typical mission of an RB-52 was to take off from *Florida*, make a simulated bomb run on *New York*, then fly over *Goose Bay*, *Labrador* to refuel. Next, they would make a simulated bomb run on

Ralph McDougal

Fairbanks, Alaska then make another one on *San Francisco* and another one on *El Paso*. After that, they would return to *Florida*.

We were trying to find out how many maintenance man-hours it took per aircraft flying hour. We found that 254 man-hours were required for every flying hour. The mission's flight took 32 hours, so it would be 8,128 maintenance man-hours for that flight.

On the B-52 and RB-52, which are exactly the same except for the load installed in the bomb bay, the wings were way out with little wingtip outrigger wheels which kept the wing stabilized while on the ground. During takeoff, those wings would go up and down and it was damaging the little wingtip wheels.

As it would take off, the wingtips would start to flap slowly. My job was to record what they were and were not doing, and how. I had to watch the landing gear clear the runway to determine the pattern of takeoff. The left rear tires, four wheels on each gear, would clear the runway first, then the right front, then the right rear—then the left front.

We had five prototypes of the B-52 and I was photo chief on number 005. When I was first assigned as photo test chief on the B-52, they sent me to *Seattle* for a two-week familiarization course at the Boeing Company.

The most impressive thing was the flexibility of the wing. The wingtip could go 19 feet up and 17 feet down.

I didn't see the sun the whole time we were in *Seattle*. On the last day, our course was over at four o'clock and our flight was at five o'clock. We didn't have time for any supper.

It was a champagne flight or something from *Seattle* to *San Francisco*. They were serving drinks, and I thought a Manhattan sounded good (never had one before). The stewardess brought me one, about four ounces, and the buddies who were with me had to help me change planes in *San Francisco*. My buddies thought it funny because I was the ranking man. I've never had another Manhattan.

A Cowboy Goes to War

Of the five prototype B-52s, number 005 was an RB, a reconnaissance bomber. It was an RB-52 because it had a reconnaissance pod that fit in the bomb bay and was equipped with photo equipment, electric countermeasure devices and electric counter-countermeasure equipment which kept any enemy from locking onto the airplane. With this equipment, we could go into enemy territory without being detected and get our reconnaissance photos.

The pod was set up with one vertical camera and two oblique cameras with telephoto lens (one shot straight down and two off to the sides), and on one run, we could cover a strip approximately fifty miles wide with no limit to the length of the run. It could be installed in any of the 52s so any of them could become a reconnaissance just by installing a pod in the bomb bay.

Progress reports involved photographic developments on base that determined the percentage of completion. These consisted of both ground photos and aerial photos.

~ ~ ~

During my time at *Eglin*, there were many crashes.

The F-101 was a very fast airplane, but if it got in a certain position at a certain speed, the airflow from the wings hit the controls on the tail and the pilot would lose control. Many times the plane crashed if they were not high enough to come out of it. Because of this problem, the F-101 had to be redlined.

We were testing the RB-57 for oscillation frequencies at high speeds, approximately 640 knots and just below the speed of sound. To do this we had a light source on the ground to determine the frequency of oscillations of the airplane.

I had been assigned a night mission and had the photo equipment all set up in the airplane when the pilot came out and met me, but he wanted to take somebody else with him as his copilot, so I stayed behind.

Ralph McDougal

When they got ready to take off, his paperwork said he should go at 15,000 feet, and he asked, "Sergeant Mac, don't you think that's too high?"

I said, "Seems high to me, but I really didn't plan it."

They took off and flew the mission, but they flew it at 1500 feet instead of 15,000 feet. When they attempted to turn the airplane at that altitude and speed, the RB-57 went into a high-speed stall with no time to recover. Before I got home, I saw the explosion when it crashed. This is one I feel bad about and don't talk about much because it still bothers me.

One time in an H-21 helicopter, the motor quit at about 500 to 600 feet, and we auto-rotated down, dropping the last 25 feet. The landing gear bent, but nobody was hurt.

When testing night flares for night photography using the new B-26, we got up to a high altitude and our flares wouldn't fire. We returned to base and when we opened the bomb bay doors—WOW. They all went off. Both banks of 30 one-million candlepower flares went off under the plane.

They weren't grounded properly when installed so they hadn't fired, but when the bomb bay doors opened they did fire because of an electrical ground situation. We were scared more than anything else because the plane contained high-octane gas and high danger of exploding.

We all got out as fast as possible and the fire department arrived. They took control then and no more danger.

~ ~ ~

On August 18, 1953, Dean was born. At 6 weeks he had to have an operation for lower pyloric stenosis. Boy, after that he really came out of it.

Almost two years later, On April 18, 1955, Mike was born. Such a cute little guy, but Dean who was weaned from the bottle and through with diapers had to be taught all over again.

Before Mike was a year old, we bought an acre of land just east of *Eglin Air Force Base* off Hwy 98. We built our first house on that land. A lot of the lumber in it came from the scrap pile at the base that we could get for 50 cents a trailer load. It wasn't much of a house, but we sure did like it, though it was much too small for seven of us.

Next we had a shell of a house built, and we finished it. That house was pretty nice.

We preferred a country home. The first one was at *Biggs Field, El Paso*, just off base at the edge of town (it's in town now). We went from there to *Newfoundlan*d, and there we rented downtown, a third story apartment. It took me awhile to find a house farther out of town. During that time I was doing a lot of flying to create the base in *Thule*, northern *Greenland*, so I was gone quite a bit.

When we came back from *Newfoundland* and arrived at *Eglin*, we lived on base a short time, then moved out east of *Eglin*. That's when we started the little town of *Seminole* where land was cheap. GIs moved in and it needed to be incorporated, so we got together and named it *Seminole*.

We built two houses out there. We didn't have anything done. I'd come home, work on the house until one or two o'clock in the morning, go to bed and then get up and go to work at the base. We'd go to the supply dump on base and for 50 cents a trailer load we could get scrap lumber. The kids built all kinds of things. Darrell had a goat named Suzy that he built a pen for.

We had ducks, chickens, and raised rabbits for a while. The gas station at the end of the street would take our dressed rabbits and they'd sell them for us. We didn't let the kids pet the rabbits we were raising to butcher. I did the butchering and Jane would take them to the store.

When we got to *Eglin*, we traded our 1953 Ford for a 1952 Buick Roadmaster because Jane thought we needed a bigger car. It was a nice car. With five kids, we made many trips to the doctor on base with cuts, scrapes, stepping on nails, colds, and all kinds of medical things.

They were active kids.

When we moved off base onto our lot in the country, both our families thought we needed some livestock: a goat Suzy, a duck, two chickens, and a dog.

I took one of Daddy's GI metal bed frames and bolted it up under the Buick with about 28 inches sticking out behind. On that we built a box with a wire front and several compartments, and that's how we got our livestock to *Florida*.

We looked like *Okies* in a four-door sedan with seven people in it and animals sticking out behind. Of course that damn goat wouldn't pee while we were moving, but when we stopped for gas and a potty stop, the goat would flood the driveway of the service station.

After a pretty long search we found a temporary mate for Suzy, but it didn't work so we went back to the source and for $10 the guy sold us that big, old billy goat. He was a shaggy thing, and the kids called him a buffalo.

When the neighbor kids coming home from the bus saw that big old ugly goat, they went home and told their parents the McDougals had a buffalo.

It soon became apparent that he couldn't cut the mustard, so we butchered him and tried to eat him, but we couldn't cut the mustard either. That meat was too tough and too rank.

We also raised rabbits. We had three does and a buck. Timing it just right, we could have the three litters born in three to five days of each other. In 30 days we would put the little ones in a fattening pen and butcher them at about 10 weeks old. The kids could name and play with the adults, but not the little ones, and that way they had no trouble eating them.

When Darrell read this manuscript, he said, "I sure never ate any of 'em!"

A Cowboy Goes to War

But he did.

We had the 3 musketeers: Suzy, the goat; Josephine the dog, and a duck that I can't remember his name. The duck was a mallard drake.

We eventually found a temporary mate for Suzy and she had twins that looked just like her.

Our four years in *Florida* were beautiful. The kids had a lot of freedom and okay schools, I got to do a lot of flying, and Jane was able to keep it all together.

Shortly before we left *Florida*, a hurricane came through and we were supposed to go to the base in a big hangar. But my thinking was, *if they evacuated all the planes out of there, why did they think we would be safe there?* So we rode it out in our house. We opened and closed windows like we were supposed to and the house withstood it fine. We didn't even lose a shingle.

The wind really blew then all of a sudden, it became completely calm, so we reversed the opening and closing of the windows. The wind came again real hard for just a short time, and then it was all over. The only real damage was our pretty white oak tree in the back yard, with about a ten inch trunk and probably 20 feet tall. It twisted off about three or four feet above the ground.

~ ~ ~

In 1956 the Air Force was in transition from prop-driven planes to jets.

We were asked to get the new planes and old planes in one formation together in flight. My photograph of this is in *LIFE* magazine, a triple-page spread. I was an Air Force photographer so it is an Air Force photo, and I was not credited. I now have a copy of that *LIFE* magazine, dated June 18, 1956.

Ralph McDougal

McDougal's Air Force photography was featured in LIFE magazine as a three pages spread though he was not personally credited for the photo. The original LIFE Magazine Vol. 40, No. 25 date of publication was June 18, 1956. The price for the publication was only 20 cents.

On the front cover the edition was billed as a 'SPECIAL EDITION.' The article was entitled: '*Air Age, Man's New Way of Life in a World Reshaped by Conquest of the Skies.*'

A Cowboy Goes to War

The jet aircraft could not fly as slow as the prop aircraft without heating up, so there had to be a separate formation of each type of plane. The picture had to be taken as the two formations passed to appear as one.

To be in a position to take the picture, we used a B-25 with the tail cone removed. A small person could crawl in and handhold a K17 camera with a 9x9 inch focal plane. With the B-25 being a prop-driven plane, we could fly off to the side of the prop plane formation and wait for the jet planes to get in the desired position.

It took a lot of coordination and dry runs to get the picture that appeared in *LIFE* magazine. When I crawled into that open hole in the tail of that B-25 it was rather scary so they strapped me in real good so that I wouldn't fall out, but I got a real surprise. Instead of trying to blow me out, I had to fight to keep from being sucked back into the plane.

1956: *Eglin Air Force Base*

Every year at *Eglin Air Force Base*, we would give a firepower demonstration to senators and government representatives to show what our combat capabilities were.

What was so interesting to me is our people would set up on the pad a nose cone from an F-84. In that nose cone was mounted a Gatling gun that would fire 300 rounds before the first empty cartridge and link hit the ground below. The ammunition is in long belts, links like a chain holding the cartridges, and the cartridge belt comes apart as the cartridges are fired. A link drops with every shot.

The significance is that they could fire so many rounds in such a short time. We couldn't use it on any aircraft where the gun was forward of the engine, because it would starve the engine of oxygen. A big ole puff of smoke would go into the engine and starve it of oxygen. That's what we did, testing what different things would do.

Ralph McDougal

Before everybody was seated in the bleachers and the firepower demonstration began, I was in the nose of an RB-57 piloted by Colonel Walsh. We flew head-on toward the grandstands at 50 feet off the ground doing 640 knots, almost at the speed of sound, to begin the demonstration.

As we passed over, I took pictures of the grandstand, and Colonel Walsh cut the throttles then headed straight up to kill our speed. We landed at *Eglin*.

By this time I had the film unloaded from the camera, and a pickup met us as soon as we got stopped on the pad. The photo lab processed the film and printed up a photo for each of the senators and representatives and delivered it to them before the firepower demonstration was over.

The quality of the picture was sufficient to identify each person in the photo. We were showing them what photo reconnaissance could do.

The firepower demonstration was outstanding, and we got good reports from the senators and representatives, but there was also a lot more to it than what I have told here.

Major DeSilva and I were ordered to *Castle Air Force Base Merced, California*. We were to test the reconnaissance pod on the B-52. On the way out, I drove through *Deming* and picked up Mamie (my mother), left her with Aunt Loney in *Riverside* and went on up to *Castle*.

We were on the ramp in our G-suits (an individual pressurization system, so if you lost aircraft pressurization you'd survive), getting ready to take off in the RB-52. A major that needed flying time came out, and I briefed him how to take my place on the flight. To make it simple, the plane blew up three miles off the end of the runway.

That ended my flying career. I then cross-trained into electronics, but I wouldn't have quit except for Jane and the family. They saw the news that my plane had gone down and they knew I was supposed to be on it.

Capt. Dudley went to the house and told Jane that the plane had gone down, but that I wasn't on board and was okay. I was a senior NCO, Master Sergeant at the time.

While I was on that trip, the floor furnace caught fire at our second new house just built at *Eglin*. Our son Darrell (at nine years old), went under the house with a hose and put it out. I didn't know about the fire until I returned home.

The reason the RB-52 exploded was each landing gear had its own power supply, and each power supply was run off the sixth stage of the jet engine and routed below the fuel tanks. The exhaust was approximately 600 degrees and a leak in the fuel tank caused the explosion.

At the crash scene, an odd thing was that the wiring and some of the instruments were rolled up in a ball about six feet high. Debris was scattered over half a mile.

This reminded me of when I was called out to take pictures of a crash scene in 1949 at the *Guadalupe Pass* between *Carlsbad* and *El Paso*. On the highest point of the pass and at the point of impact, we found the pilot's billfold and his testicles. The plane was a P-51. There was quite a burn area and debris over the hill. He was only 10 feet low of clearing the pass.

My last official mission as aerial photographer was testing the RB-66 at high altitude, 55,000 feet, dropping flares. We could see three states, *Florida*, *Alabama*, and *Georgia*. It was fascinating.

We used a K17 camera (12-inch lens), K18 (18-inch lens), and K40 (40-inch focal length lens) and was 40 inches tall, 9x18 inch photo plane.

The prototype RB-66 that we were testing did not test out. So it went back to the manufacturer for modification. They replaced a bicycle landing gear with a tricycle gear, and it was successful, but that was proven after I had already left *Florida*. We were all so sad to leave *Florida*.

We gave our dog, Josephine and our duck to people down the street. Before we left, we had a community meeting and named our community *Seminole*, because the area used to be *Seminole* Indian country.

I got orders for *Lowry Air Force Base* in *Denver*, *Colorado*, to go into electronics training, a new career. By then we were driving a 1955 Chevy station wagon.

Ralph and Jane's five children,
Dwayne, Darrell, Debbie, Dean and Mike.

Chapter 29
Electronics School

1953—1957: *Lowry Air Force Base - Denver, Colorado*

Upon arrival in *Denver*, housing was not available so we lived in a motel several weeks until we could get base housing. While in the motel someone gave us a real nice Boxer puppy.

After about four days with five kids and a new puppy, Jane said, "That is it!"

So Chief went back to where he came from.

While in *Denver*, Jane took her GED and passed it high enough that she could go right into college. She always wanted to go to college, but she never got there. She went to work for a company called Financial Industrial Funds and that started her education and experience in finance.

We traded our 1955 Chevy in on a 1957 Plymouth 9-passenger station wagon, yellow trimmed in white. Boy, what a vehicle. It had the Fury engine with twin four barrel carburetor and dual ignition.

If Jane couldn't drive 100 mph or better she didn't want to drive. She could be driving along at about 80 and the kids would holler, "Mommy ... hit the fast button!" She would push the pedal to the metal and set them back in their seats. It could pass anything but a gas station.

Lowry was a good assignment. The kids had good schools and daycare. Also, Jane could work and take care of our family.

Denver is in some very pretty country and has an outstanding zoo and natural history museum. During Christmas, the lights were out of this world.

Ralph McDougal

Things were very tight money-wise that Christmas, but we all remember it well because of the Christmas tree which made our Christmas that year. We were just barely squeakin' by on GI pay.

I went to electronics school and had a part-time job selling Nutrilite food supplements, but I was not a very good salesman.

We hadn't had our new Plymouth very long when Daddy got tangled up with a high voltage power line and we took a 10-day emergency leave. Daddy was in pretty bad shape and we almost flew to *Deming* in that new Plymouth.

While at the school in *Denver*, I got orders for *Malmstrom Air Force Base, Great Falls, Montana*.

Chapter 30
NCOIC of Armament & Electronics

1958: *Malmstrom Air Force Base, Montana*

Upon being assigned to *Malmstrom Air Force Base*, I was a level three trainee on the F-89 jet called the Scorpion. It had an E-9 radar system in it, and we were given six weeks of OJT (on-the-job training). Upon completing the course, I was made a level five.

Because they needed an NCOIC in Armament and Electronics, they made me a level seven and put me in charge. My rank MSGT E-7 (Master Sergeant) didn't change, a rank I had been since September 2, 1944. At the time, it was a top rank of the enlisted men.

After I made supervisor, I immediately started training to go to the William Tell Competition, a live-fire fighter aircraft competition held every two years representing all Air Defense Command (ADC) units to see who could have the best firing record. I had quite a number of OJTs to complete and a squadron of F-89s to get ready for the competition, so in the summer of 1958, we took the squadron to *Yuma, Arizona* to compete.

It was very hot and miserable, but we had an enjoyable time because we won the William Tell. We set a record for the air defense command, and I had the privilege of doing that twice in my lifetime.

I received a 30-day leave between assignments, so just before *Malmstrom*, we went to *New Mexico*. Mawmaw and Pawpaw had the railroad section at *Hermanas*. We left Dwayne and Darrell with the folks. Jane, Debbie, Dean, Mike and I went on to *Great Falls*. Mawmaw and Pawpaw put Dwayne and Darrell in school at *Columbus* for about two months before bringing them on up to *Great Falls*. There was a house ready for us on base when we got there.

That summer, Pawpaw took his vacation and they brought the boys up to *Malmstrom* for us.

The military had some small RV trailers set up *in Glacier National Park* so I reserved one for the weekend. We really had a good time but it was cold, even if it was summer.

The first morning after we got there, I got up early and went up the stream a little ways and caught fresh trout for breakfast. Pawpaw and I were trying to light the Coleman stove and it caught fire and was flaming up big so I just grabbed it and threw it out the door. I had on long sleeves so I only got my hands blistered and singed a bit. With Pawpaw's help we got it going, and, no, it did not come back inside.

We all piled into the station wagon and headed out to see what we could see. There was a big mountain goat about halfway up the bluff, just standing there looking at us. So we stopped and we gawked at that goat in amazement as he hung onto the side of that bluff. We saw a lot of wildlife and at that time the park had 150 glaciers. I think there is less than 50 now.

The country around *Great Falls* was very different, a lot of rolling hills covered with wheat fields. The little canyons that run toward the *Missouri River* are called coulees. A chinook wind could come up very fast and the temperature could change fast from below 0 degrees to above freezing in a couple of hours. We sure didn't like that. While driving around we discovered a good-sized beaver pond that the kids liked to swim in, but I think they froze more than they swam.

The falls at *Great Falls* disappointed the kids. They weren't very tall, but a long way across. They were on the *Missouri River*. What was so interesting to me was the spring a short ways above the falls that was putting out 4,000,000 gallons of fresh water a minute. It made up most of the river at that point.

Our close friends at *Malmstrom* were Paul and Mary Drawn with daughter Barbara and little brother Butch. Both Dwayne and Darrell thought Barbara was special. Darrell didn't say much, but Dwayne did. The boys were ten and eleven years old, so I guess they were growing up.

~ ~ ~

Montana was okay and we did enjoy it, but we wanted to get closer to home. I managed to get transferred to *Davis-Monthan Air Force Base* in *Tucson, Arizona.* It snowed in *Tucson* the day we arrived.

Of course housing was hard to find, so again we used the GI Bill and bought a new 3-bedroom house. We made the carport into a fourth bedroom for Dwayne and Darrell.

Our stay in *Tucson* was rather short.

We had to give up our nine-passenger station wagon because gas mileage was terrible, and got a Studebaker President. It was small, but got good gas mileage and traveled well.

Before leaving *Tucson*, we bought an older model International three-quarter ton pickup, orange with black fenders. It was good for hauling material and running around the desert. It helped move us to *Kirtland Air Force Base* in *Albuquerque, New Mexico.*

At first we got quarters in an old base house, but a short time later we got quarters in the new Wherry Housing Project. That was a nice house. A four bedroom with all new appliances and a nice yard.

The kids were growing up.

One of the men from the fire department got me a couple of gallons of fire engine red paint so the kids and I painted our pickup fire-engine red. It wasn't a very good job, but it sure was bright. We traded our Studebaker in on a station wagon so we had a little more room and we still had our pickup.

We did a lot of driving in the mountains, as well as to and from *Deming* and *Canutillo*. The boys and I left the girls at home and took the red pickup to spend some time together in the mountains then met the girls at Mawmaw and Pawpaw's in *Canutillo*.

Ralph McDougal

We were in our new house on Halloween and were all ready for trick or treaters. After the first two or three kids came to the door, we scared them so bad that we didn't have any more come to the door. Our kids sure had a lot of candy to eat.

As I remember it, my job at *Kirtland* wasn't so stressful and I spent a lot of time with the family.

Before Christmas in 1959, I got orders for *Goose Bay, Labrador*. While on leave before going overseas, Pawpaw died of a massive heart attack. I had my leave extended long enough to see Pawpaw buried and to get things in order for Mawmaw.

Chapter 31
Labrador

1959—1963: *Goose Bay Air Force Base*

In late fall of 1959, the family and I arrived in *Goose Bay, Labrador*, during a snowstorm, and we saw a lot more snow after that.

They had a three-bedroom house ready for us to stay in until a four-bedroom was available which didn't take long to get. Our first order of business was to get issued arctic clothing for the whole family and to attend arctic survival training, about a week.

Our car couldn't be shipped up until the ice broke up the next summer, so we got in a lot of walking. Automatic transmissions didn't work well up there because of the cold. To be able to start the car in the morning, I had to keep it plugged into an electric outlet to keep the engine warm so the oil wouldn't congeal.

Nighttime was almost 24 hours. It never gets totally dark during the day, but there isn't sunlight. As a result, our extension cords from the shop kept disappearing, so I went to the commander and got permission to order the material to build up a bunch of those cords so the guys could steal them. It worked.

Mike's big white tomcat, Snowball, had to be shipped separately and cost $31, which I thought was too much, but I was glad we did it. He was a real comfort to the whole family. Snowball (the tomcat) was such a pretty thing, but we decided to dye him scarlet. It took three of us to do it, and all four of us came out pastel pink.

Of course Snowball was the most beautiful. A pastel pink tomcat really turned some heads and made some people wonder about their drinking. A few months before we left *Goose Bay*, Snowball just disappeared.

Ralph McDougal

Goose Bay is where we made a toboggan run. We built our own toboggan in the basement, and we built it heavy.

It was great going down the hill, but really tough bringing it back up. The hill we were on was pretty steep and about 100 yards long. We clocked our toboggan at top speed of 69mph. When it crested a small bump midway down the run, we'd go airborne, but then we'd come back down with a *hulff* and end up going 69mph by the time we got to the frozen river below.

On that hillside, the snow had blown in and covered the pine trees. They didn't grow very tall up there, only about 20 feet high. Once, Darrell sped down, flew airborne and lost his glasses. We couldn't find them then, but the next spring we found them hanging in a pine tree pretty much none the worse for wear.

When it was more than 20 below zero degrees Fahrenheit, the Air Police would come out and tell us to stay inside, because after that, we couldn't tell if it got colder. About mid-December, it would go below zero and we wouldn't see zero again till the middle of March.

We spent four years up there.

The kids would shovel out an area about 50 feet in diameter with snow shovels then call the fire department to come and fill it with water to make a little ice skating rink. One time when the kids were ice skating, Darrell fell down. A girl came by and fell over him and broke his arm.

In the latter part of September, the bay would freeze up. Once, we made a wooden ice shack and drug it out on the ice with the pickup. Then we cut a hole in the ice to fish through, and the housing maintenance people would run an electric line out to us so we would have light.

During the daytime in the winter, the sun might come up for an hour or so. It wasn't rainy and cloudy much of the time, but we got 16 feet of snow each year.

We had snow blowers, huge machines that would blow snow quite a few feet up and out. We called them *airman eaters* because an incident happened where an airman came out of a club intoxicated and passed out in the snow. The snow blower just chopped him up, and that's why we called them airman eaters.

All vehicles that used the roads were required to have a high antenna with a flag on it so at intersections, drivers could see somebody coming, because we drove in trenches of snow. It didn't work all that well, but it was some help. The cars weren't very plentiful up there because there was only six miles of road, and the cars almost filled the whole trench.

Storms would come in every three or four days, snow like the dickens and clear up for several days then it would storm again.

We lived in two-story buildings, and snow would be halfway up the upstairs windows. We had to keep our doorway dug out. They kept the roads pretty well clear.

In the ice shack, we put in a 55-gallon drum with a hole cut in the side. We put a big rock in it and put a chimney on it.

When an airplane was out on the runway, it got real cold, but when we brought it in for maintenance the cold fuel would expand and we'd catch it in drip pans. That excess fuel is what we used to heat our ice shacks.

The oil barrel outside the shack was kept up high enough that it would drip onto the rock by gravity and it would keep the shack toasty warm.

We caught smelt, little fish three to eight inches long. After we caught the first one, we took its throat out and laced it on our hook then we could fish all night. Smelt is a soft fish we cleaned with our hands.

We'd have to chip the ice out every time we went fishing, but it didn't freeze all the way to the top and it was easy to chip it out. By the time spring came, the ice was about seven feet thick.

One day we decided to have a *live off the land* thing. Mike was seven and the older boys thirteen or fourteen.

Dwayne caught some nice trout from a stream, and we had blueberries and cranberries with the fish. We also killed a porcupine and a ptarmigan with a BB gun. They fixed it up and we had a real neat meal—Jane, me, our kids, and some other kids.

Moon Mullins was a chef, one of the sergeants up on an isolated tour. He did the cooking for our off-the-land dinner. He was a typical chef, big and fat.

He had a small car that he demonstrated to the boys how he could drive out into the parking lot, spin three circles on the ice and come out where he wanted. He looked like he was just about as big as the car.

When he left to go home, he left the car for the boys.

Jane always would rather have kids visit our house than have our kids at someone else's house.

We did enjoy *Goose Bay*. We had a good commissary with plenty of fruits and vegetables.

Jane got hungry for Mexican food and went to the commissary officer and said, "Lots of us here like Mexican food."

They brought in tortillas, chili and enchilada sauce, all canned, of course. Lots of people enjoyed that.

~ ~ ~

While in *Goose Bay*, an OIC (Officer in Charge) brought in a first lieutenant and we called a meeting for him to get acquainted with the people. He immediately started cussing them.

When he started cussing, I stood up and said, "You cannot cuss my men!"

He told me, "I will have you court-martialed for insubordination!"

I reached over, picked up the phone and called the base commander, Colonel Jones, and said to him, "The lieutenant and I are having a problem. We'd like to have a meeting with you."

The colonel said, "Let me speak with the lieutenant."

Colonel Jones told him to come up to the office and bring me with him. The lieutenant thought he was taking me up there to be court-martialed. When we got there, the colonel asked what my complaint was. I told him the lieutenant was cussing the men and didn't know what he was talking about.

After I told the colonel my complaint, he turned to the lieutenant and asked, "Is that correct?"

The lieutenant replied, "Yes, but—"

The colonel said, "That's enough. You see that desk in the next room? That will be your desk. You will still be OIC of Armament and Electronics and you will sign the paperwork that Sgt. Mac sends you. But you will *not* go down to the shop."

So that's the way it was for a year, until the lieutenant rotated.

Sgt. Mac's Card Game:

While in a supervisor's position, problems of all kinds would come up, whether it was with many individuals or with only a few. Problems that were work-related, home, and individual difficulties, disputes between workers or even between groups of people. Many times it could be quite easy to solve or at least obtain something to go on if it needed to be taken further.

I would call the person or persons together and tell them I wanted to play a card game, "Lay the cards on the table."

First, why are we here? When this was agreed upon, I would ask them one at a time to lay their cards on the table. *"No interruptions, please*, you will get your turn."

This part was a bit hard to control, but I was the ranking man and the one to make the decision on the outcome.

Ralph McDougal

After all the information was on the table, I would ask for a few moments of quiet for each one to think about what they had heard and how or what should be done to best complete our mission.

We might have a cup of coffee. Each one would then get a chance to voice their opinion.

Then it's time for discussion and possibly a resolution. I would then make the decision with the understanding that if they weren't pleased with it, they had my permission to take it to the Officer in Charge. I would make an attempt to turn the situation so they felt like their input would improve the conditions for accomplishing the mission. We very seldom had to go to the OIC.

Many times he would sit in on the card game, but I preferred he didn't because they would feel intimidated.

Decisions could be to transfer to a different job or section or even removal from the section.

~ ~ ~

'Moreover if thy brother shall trespass against thee, go and tell him his fault between thee and him alone: if he shall hear thee, thou hast gained thy brother.

But if he will not hear thee, then take with thee one or two more, that in the mouth of two or three witnesses every word may be established.

And if he shall neglect to hear them, tell it unto the church: but if he neglect to hear the church, let him be unto thee as an heathen man and a publican.'
(Matthew 18:15-17) *The Holy Bible*, King James Version.

We were having a dining-in of the officers and men of the 59th Fighter Wing *Frigadendeau*, and we had to toast first where the bottle never touches the table until it's empty, and then get another one.

The chaplain didn't get there so we waited about five minutes then Colonel Jones got up and asked Sgt. Mac to say the blessing.

A Cowboy Goes to War

It scared me to death.

I had no idea what to say, so I was greatly relieved that the chaplain made it for the benediction. There were well over 500 people there.

~ ~ ~

At first, my job was very stressful because I had spent ten years before, helping set up the detection and early warning system in the artic to alert people of an incoming bogey (incoming target).

Goose Bay was set up with the fighter airplanes to prevent those bogeys from reaching the United States, but when I got to *Goose Bay*, there wasn't a plane (F-102s) that could be assured of firing a missile, even the planes on alert duty.

My job was stressful because I would sign a Red X on the aircraft form, which meant that airplane could not be flown until the Red X was cleared. I was called on the carpet many times, but I figured it only took five minutes to get a chewing, and I felt like I was doing what was right for my country.

It took us quite a few months to get it up to par, but three years later we won William Tell Competition again. I didn't go this time. I sent Chuck Culmsee, my top-notch technician.

I didn't do the work, I just made it possible for them to do it. I spent many long hours day and night in the hangar and on the flight line.

We did get in some fishing and spent some really quality family time together.

Most of my GIs were at *Goose Bay* on an isolated tour. That meant they were up there for one year with no family and almost nothing to do but work and go to the club. The people on isolated tours were housed in huge barracks we called the *Tiltin' Hilton* because the foundation sank on one side, causing the building to slightly tilt because it was built on a sandbar.

Jane became a den mother and we never knew how many of the guys would show up to share our home and family.

We got to know Randy Neff whose father was in charge of the rescue dog teams. So the kids got to know a bit about dog teams. I think they chased the dogs more than they rode on the sled.

In the summertime when the ice thawed, there were some pretty nice ponds down below the hill. The kids that were together most were our five, Bruce Joham, and Randy Neff. The kids got four 55-gallon barrels and some boards and made a raft to go on one of the bigger ponds, and it worked pretty well.

When winter came, it froze and was covered with about 20 feet of snow.

Finally, summer did come and the kids went down to break their raft out of the ice. In the process, Debbie fell through the ice. That day Bruce Joham was the hero because he pulled Debbie out of the water. She was a cold little girl, but she was one tough little dude.

In the spring when the ice broke up on the river, big thick blocks of ice would come floating down. Dwayne, Darrell and I would jump on one of those blocks, and as we floated down the river, we would jump from block to block. It was great sport.

The river was getting close to the bay at this point, so the ice was flowing very slowly.

~ ~ ~

We hadn't been in *Goose Bay* long until Mawmaw joined us and stayed until we came home.

When we got ready to come home, we ordered a new Chevy nine-passenger station wagon to be picked up in *New Jersey*.

As we left *Goose Bay* in July, the snow was still in large banks on each side of the runway. We left *Goose Bay* in our winter clothes and nearly burned up when we got to *New Jersey*.

A Cowboy Goes to War

I had a lot of leave time coming, so I took 30 days leave. In our new Chevy nine-passenger wagon we headed for *New Mexico* to see family.

We had been away overseas for almost four years.

Mamie & Luther "Hamp" McDougal.

Chapter 32
Family

1962: *Richard Gebaur Air Force Base - Kansas City, Missouri*

After a great leave, I reported in to *Richard Gebaur Air Force Base* near *Grandview, Missouri*, a suburb of *Kansas City*. We hadn't been on base very long until we found two acres off base with a large mobile home on it, and of course we started building on. Our place was very pretty.

The property was long and narrow with the back part on a hill with an apple tree on it. The slope of the hill down to the house was covered with wild strawberries, small but very sweet.

We didn't have to plant a lawn, all we had to do was mow it. The lawn was beautiful and took very little water, but damn! It was full of chiggers. We also had a lot of fireflies and birds.

This is where our kids started to high school and where they got their drivers licenses. My family was growing up.

Prior to leaving *Goose Bay*, Dean's teacher called Jane and told her that Dean was retarded and she wanted to see Jane. Jane went prepared to mop the floor with this teacher because Dean was a sharp little guy.

I got Jane calmed down by telling her we were leaving very shortly, so we would get him enrolled with good teachers.

Upon arrival at *Richard Gebaur*, I went down to the school and told them the story and asked them to assign Dean to the best teacher they could possibly give him. It was Mrs. See, and she was the best. Dean started coming out of it, and he became an Honor Roll student for the rest of his school life.

While on leave in *New Mexico*, we told the family about the situation with Dean.

My sister Muriel, a longtime school teacher, looked at her husband Arvel and said, "I think he needs a horse."

At that time Muriel and Arvel were raising horses as well as her teaching school.

Arvel piped up and said, "I have a neat little palomino mare that is ready to be weaned. That's what he needs."

So I asked, "How in the world would I get her back to *Missouri?*"

My brother Luther, with a big smile, said, "I've got a stock rack you can borrow!"

We put the stock rack on the pickup and covered it with a tarp. We got April in there and headed for *Missouri*.

A comical side of this was that one of the kids rode back there with her all the time, and when they would call for a coke we would pass it out the window back to them. Onlookers could see the horse, but not the child, and each one was left with a big question mark.

That horse and Mrs. See changed Dean's entire life. He retired on his own ranch with his own horses in *Gila National Forest, New Mexico.*

Mike's teacher called to see how Mike was (I think it was during his second grade, but I'm not positive) and I said, "He's doing fine. Have you got a problem?"

She replied, "He hasn't been to school for two weeks."

That's when we began to investigate. He didn't lie to me. He had been going to the lake every day. The teacher scolded him about a math problem and he said he didn't like it. We didn't have any problems getting him to go back. As far as I know everything was okay.

He knew all the frogs in the lake.

Every year we'd go out and cut our own Christmas trees, and we were in a lot of different places!

Ralph McDougal

Jane went to work in Civil Service and finance, and they were setting up their first computers. A computer at that time took up a whole air-conditioned room and many employees at desks around it. Jane did well and liked her work, and that prepared her for future finance work in Civil Service.

Ralph, Jane and children

Chapter 33
Panama Riots

1964: Air Defense Command

Our Air Defense Command (ADC) area of protection was the southeastern quarter of the U.S. and included the *Caribbean Islands* and *Panama*. I was stationed at *Richard Gebaur Air Force Base* in *Kansas City*, but we had six alert airplanes stationed in *Key West*, *Florida*. About all I did was furnish airplanes for *Key West*.

I was the noncommissioned officer in charge (NCOIC) of Armament (missiles) and Electronics, making sure the missiles were firing. Our mission was to go anywhere we needed to recover the airplanes that were launched, and be ready to re-launch in 12 hours. The idea was that if we had an attack, within 12 hours we could recover the airplanes and go on to the next mission.

We learned a lot on the first trip down. They assigned us three C-130s to load our equipment on in preparation. I had a list of all the equipment I needed to perform my basic mission, but I didn't have foresight enough to divide it equally between all three planes.

I had all my transmitter-receiver (TR) units on one airplane, and it emergency-landed in *Nicaragua*. After that, I (and the whole Air Force) learned to divide up the necessary equipment between the planes. We made it to *Key West* all right and launched our first mission within the 12-hour period.

The mission was to show force, not to do any firing. We would launch two airplanes every hour and they'd fly the main street of *Panama City* with bomb bay doors open at low altitude. They'd fly the length of the *Panama Canal* then fly back and do the same thing on the way back. I didn't need my TR units and I sure was glad of that. The news media reported that we were strafing the streets, but that was absolutely not true.

In *Panama City* I discovered a delicacy was roasted Iguana tails. That fascinated me. I got to thinking about it and called the *Kansas City Zoo* to see if they would like me to bring some iguanas home because they were all over the beach. They said yes, so I attempted to catch iguanas, but all I got was the tail. They would shed the tail. The last part is tiny, but the part to eat was about two feet long. Since I ended up with just the tails, I got some Panamanians that worked on base to catch me some. I asked for two males and two females.

The Panamanians caught four of them for me, a big male seven feet, two inches long and the other just under seven feet. One of the females was six feet and seven inches, and the other six feet. They weren't very wide.

I went to the carpenter shop on base and got a sheet of plywood and put 1x12s on it like bookshelves then covered the front with mesh wire. The *Kansas City Zoo* was there to meet us and take care of all the customs and the paperwork. I didn't have anything more to do with it after we got home.

On that same trip coming back, I tried to bring back a stalk of bananas in some of the electronic equipment. I gave a dollar for that stalk, almost 100 pounds (3½-4 feet long). But it smelled so good, the customs agent found it and struggled it into his pickup. So my kids got to see it, but they didn't get to eat any of it.

It was in *Panama* that my dizzy spells started. Once I went 72 hours straight trying to get everything done. I've had dizzy spells on and off ever since and get motion sick, nauseous and vomiting. However, I may go for months without symptoms.

We weren't supposed to get off base and fraternize with the Panamanians. It was a wartime situation as far as we were concerned, but the girls came up the beach and came to us around the fence at the beach on the edge of the base. There were a lot of sharks there and they had fenced off an area for swimming out into the water so the sharks couldn't get in.

The girls came around the fence to meet the guys. When it was time to go home, three married men were found to have gonorrhea. There was no doubt it would be the end of those marriages.

I went to the commander and asked if we couldn't Red X (make not flyable) the plane in maintenance for three days. What we did was to find a part that would take three days to ship it in. The guys would take penicillin and they would be okay by the time they got home. The flight surgeon was in on this too.

As NCOIC, even though there was a commander, I was the one who executed the thing. The NCOIC is the go-between for the officers and the enlisted personnel. Officers don't mess with the enlisted men, they tell us what needs to be done and we get it done with the men and supplies that are available. Enlisted men didn't mess with me as the NCOIC because I outranked them. NCOIC is the best rank to have.

The officer may just be a figurehead.

In *Kansas City*, I had 140 men under me, but I didn't take them all to *Panama*. We had one barracks set up for my people. Out of the 140, I don't remember how many I took from *Kansas City*, probably close to 100 people, but we had 36 airplanes to take care of.

There were NCOICs over each branch, Maintenance, Communications, etc., and several of us over the different things. Some had separate NCOICs for Armament and Electronics, but my last two outfits, I was NCOIC of both Armament and Electronics, at *Goose Bay*—59th Fighter Wing Air Defense Command (ADC) and at *Richard Gebaur*.

In 1964, I was deployed to *Panama* twice during the Panama riots. During my second deployment, I started getting dizzy spells that would make me seasick. Then my life changed. For the next two years, I was in and out of the hospital trying to find out what was wrong with me.

Ralph McDougal

They couldn't find out what was wrong, so on 1 Sept 1966, the U.S. Air Force retired me and said, "Learn to live with it."

I am still trying to learn to live with it. I am still quite limited with what I can do, but with some changes, we have still had a good family life. I believe the Lord had a lot to do with it. Only with His help have I made it.

All the kids did well in school. Dwayne went into the Navy. Darrell went into the Army. Debbie, Dean and Mike were still in school.

In a way, *Missouri* was a very good memory in our lives. We then retired.

When I was told that I was being retired, Big Black Bart, my assistant in the office, said, "If you're going, I'm going too."

He went down and put in his retirement papers also.

When I retired my rank was Chief Master Sergeant on Duty, but because I had stayed in the Officer's Reserve, I retired at the highest rank held, which was a Major.

I retired on September 1, 1966, and had honorably served for twenty-three years, two months, and three days.

Chapter 34
Family Life in Retirement

1967–1974: *White Sands Missile Range*

I was discharged from the Air Force and told to go home and learn to live with vestibular neuronitis and told I could expect a life of 6 to 12 years, so we decided we needed to go someplace and dig in.

We started in *Las Cruces* and that Christmas was a lean one, but really a very special one.

The kids and I gathered up gourds, and Dean painted them high-gloss silver or gold as bulbs on the Christmas tree. For decoration he took a big tumbleweed and sprayed it silver. We got a Yucca plant and bought a bag of multi-colored gumdrops and put a gumdrop on the point of each Yucca leaf.

Most of that Christmas was homemade.

For a short while, I got a job as mailman.

I had a very interesting thing happen while I was a mailman. Of course, everybody was playing tricks on me because as a disabled veteran, I went ahead of them on the job.

On my mail route was a big bay window. After a few days, I came up to that house with the big window and my eyes got big because inside lay a woman and a child with not a stitch of clothes on.

She looked at me, smiled and waved so I smiled, waved and delivered her mail. Then I got out of there.

My mailman career didn't last more than two weeks.

In January of 1967, I went to work for Dynalectron at *Holloman Air Force Base* near *Alamogordo, New Mexico*, so we moved to *Alamogordo*.

Another interesting thing happened shortly after I retired when Jane and I and two other couples were at the ranch—Dyar and Nelda and Luther and Dorothy. We said we'd watch the place for Nadine while she went to an art conference at *Ruidoso*.

We drove up to the big gap to check things out, and Nadine's bulls and May's bulls had been fighting through the fence and wrecked a large section of fence.

Luther, Dyar and I started to put the fence back like we did when we were kids by tying the wires the same way, kind of a déjà vu thing. When I was a kid, Daddy went away from home to work and I was pretty much in charge of lots of things. Luther and Dyar worked a lot with me at the time.

The next few years were very busy. Son Dwayne in the Navy, son Darrell went to *Alaska* to be with Chuck Culmsee. Daughter Debbie, son Dean and son Mike were in school.

My mom died which was a very big blow to all of us. She not only had us, she sustained us.

Son Darrell joined the Army and was sent to *Fort Bliss* for electronics school. Jane was working in finance at *White Sands* where she met GiGi.

Son Darrell brought some of his friends up from *Fort Bliss* on weekends. John was one of them, and Jane brought GiGi home with her one weekend.

Dwayne got home from the Navy and in very short order, I had a daughter-in-law. Mary, one of Debbie's high school friends became Dwayne's wife. A daughter-in-law GiGi who became Darrell's wife and a son-in-law John who became Debbie's husband. It was all so fast that it left Jane and me in a spin. This all happened in 1968.

Now the begetting began. Dwayne and Mary begat Tammy and DeeDee, granddaughters. Dwayne and Vera begat Stephany and Kimberly granddaughters. Darrell and GiGi begat Christina and Mike grandkids. Debbie and John begat Charlie and Kacy grandkids. Dean and Sarah begat Dirk and Matty grandkids. Mike and Chris begat Alex and Emily grandkids.

A Cowboy Goes to War

And the begetting continued.

After I retired, I worked for Dynalectron, a private contractor on *White Sands Missile Range*, from 1967-1974. At first I was in Research and Development and worked myself out of what I really enjoyed doing, building the Fixed Camera Control System (a big computer) and hands-on electronics. I couldn't refuse promotion because there was money in it and with kids at home and other expenses, I needed the extra money.

We built the fixed camera control system computer while I was an A-Tech. Ed Williams was the engineer who designed it. He didn't like the hands-on work and I did.

He would put a block diagram on the board and I filled in the components, parts and values. The system was to control multiple cameras from the distance of 15 miles, on two wires. We could start the cameras, stop them and monitor the film speeds and the amount of film used.

One of the basic missions we did was testing the Maverick missile. It was a primary weapon against tanks, and what they wanted was to see a missile hitting a tank in slow motion and how it broke up. So we set up three 35mm cameras made with a rotating lens.

Each camera had 1200 feet of film on it. And the run time on each camera was 1.2 seconds, so we adjusted the start time on each camera so it was 144,000 frames per second. The cameras would come on in sequence, so as soon as the first one went off, the second one was already up to speed. That gave us a total of 3 seconds.

The missile was fired from the F-111 at a range of about two or three miles out from the target.

We had to adjust with the fixed camera control system so the camera would be on when the missile hit the tank. The tank has really thick armor plating, and we could show the missile touching and entering then breaking up following entry into the tank.

We had thermometers to see what the temperature would be inside the tank, and the maximum reached was 900 degrees Fahrenheit.

Ralph McDougal

The tremendous success of the photos of the Maverick missile hitting the tank and breaking up as it entered, started a complete chain of events. The company created a Fixed Camera Section. And of course, there were a number of people who put in for the job as supervisor. They all had more seniority than I did, but I was made supervisor of the section.

Many of the things I did while there are interesting, such as the *Athena Program*, the *Minuteman Missile* test and the *Cruise Missile*.

Athena Program

This program was set up to determine what materials to use on the nose of the shuttle spacecraft, because it was having trouble with material by notwithstanding the heat during atmosphere reentry. To do this, we fired the missile out into space from *Green River, Utah*, using four different materials on its nosecone.

We had cameras set up on the launch in *Green River*, and we had open-exposure-type cameras set up all around *White Sands Missile Range*, southern *New Mexico*. *White Sands Missile Range* is about the size of *Rhode Island*, so that meant the cameras were pretty well scattered out to get the missile reentry from many different angles.

The cameras we used were preset predicting entry positions of the missile and used film on glass plates which had less distortion than other types of film. It was color film. As the missile started reentry, we opened the shutter and let it stay open until the missile landed. This happened on a very dark time of the night so the stars and the missile would show up on the film. The missile looks like a streak coming clear across the film.

The film was taken to *White Sands* for processing. I would pick up the film and take it to Physical Science Laboratory (PSL) at New Mexico State University (NMSU). They used star maps to determine the trajectory of the missile, and at any time during its trajectory, they could tell its position within six inches.

The color film allowed for the position and temperature changes of the nose materials to be recorded on film as it came through different levels of atmosphere.

My job at PSL was to determine if I had the quality of photos they needed to do their job. A problem we had was if they fired the missile at the wrong time, the moonlight would interfere with the picture quality.

I complained to them about the firing time because it deteriorated the quality, so the physicist in *California* sent word back for me to set the time. I went to town and got me a Farmer's Almanac, which had a detailed pattern on the moon positions then I set the missions at a time when the moon wouldn't interfere.

Eventually they decided on the ceramic material for the nosecone.

The missiles weren't always on target and several of them landed other than at the *White Sands Missile Range*. One outstanding incident I remember, a missile landed in *Juarez, Mexico*. We could track where it was going, but we had no control over it.

I don't know how they did it, but the government quieted an international incident.

Minuteman Missile

The testing of the *Minuteman Missile* had included parts being tested, but not the entire system as one unit being detonated so one was set up in *White Sands Missile Range*, up near *Trinity Site*, the first atomic explosion site.

We spent weeks getting our camera set up so we could get in detail the explosion to include the shock wave, breakup, distribution of shrapnel and extent of shrapnel range. In other words, the destructive power of a non-nuclear warhead.

When everything was ready and the date set for the detonation, we arrived on site very early in the morning. It was colder in *New Mexico* than I'd ever seen it before, thirteen degrees Fahrenheit. The

Ralph McDougal

detonation time was delayed several hours due to difficulty getting equipment set up and generators running because of the cold.

To detect the shock wave, we took condoms filled with argon gas and placed them down the length of the missile at one-foot intervals so when the shock wave hit they would glow and we could tell how the shock wave traveled through the missile. A very sexy missile. It worked well. The mission was a success, even though we lost a number of cameras due to film breakage.

We had almost daily missions that were much smaller than the *Athena* and *Minuteman*, and I ended up Photographic Supervisor of the Dynalectron Missile Range at *White Sands*.

~ ~ ~

We sold our place in *Alamogordo* and moved onto ten acres out west of *Alamogordo* where we really had some good family times, but our kids got scattered and Jane and I tried a bit of RV'ing. After a while, we came back and built a house across the road from the ten acres then eventually sold the house and the other land.

We did a lot of playing and building and water witching, deer hunting. Just plain good family fun. I sure did and do love my family. I am so proud of all of them.

While in *Alamogordo* and our grandkids were young, we got to spend a lot of time with them, those were some very special times.

One time we were headed west on 1st Street with the six grandkids in the back of the pickup, Charlie, Kacy, Tammy, Dee Dee, Chris, and Mike. The people in the cars around us were acting strange, so we looked back and the kids were throwing fingers at everybody and just laughing up a storm.

One late spring when Darrell's son Mike was about four or five years old, a group of us went goat hunting up on *Pasture Ridge* in the *Sacramento Mountains* near *Alamogordo*. When we got parked, I was in one of my dizzy spells so I told the boys to go on and I would just walk around the pickup a bit.

A Cowboy Goes to War

They headed off down the canyon and I was going to walk over where I could sit down and watch them.

I hadn't gone far until I spotted two little fawns hiding in a big clump of grass. I laid my gun down, sneaked up and picked up one of the little deer. It was a little buck just a few days old all dressed in his spotted youth. I called the boys (they hadn't gotten very far) and they came to where I was and Mike loved that little deer. We played with him a while then turned him loose.

Mike could hardly stand for us to turn him loose and he cried and fussed the rest of the trip.

Charlie and Kacy were spending the summer with Jane and me, and Charlie was getting very good riding his bicycle so we took the tractor and built a course with bumps and turns and so on. Charlie was good at riding that course. He'd ride as soon as he got up in the morning. He went flying around and went over one of the jumps and sailed right over a four-foot rattlesnake. It got exciting for a little bit.

We were working on the skirting of the trailer house and had moved the steps away from the back door. Kacy decided to join us and came running out that door—OOPS, no step. She broke her collar bone.

While living in that trailer house, son Mike was living with us. A family of skunks moved in under the trailer. Mike and I built a figure-four trap and set it. The next morning, we had a skunk.

Mike said, "Now what?"

I said, "Pick him up real quick by the tail before he can get his back feet set and he can't spray you."

He got him picked up, okay, then he said, "Now what do I do?"

I said, "I don't know, Mike."

I went to work with Mike standing there holding that skunk up by the tail. When I got home I asked him what he did.

He said, "I kept him swinging in a circle and held him out the window of my pickup and drove out away from the house, and while driving threw him out into some weeds."

Ralph McDougal

The first year we moved out west of *Alamogordo*, we had the best garden I have ever seen. Everything grew bigger and prettier than you can imagine. The next year it was just about normal and the third year it just wasn't very good and the fourth year forget it.

The water was salty and killed the soil. So very disheartening. A few plants would grow fairly well, but not the ones we wanted. So much for my farming. I raised kids better than anything else.

We tried cutting wood and selling it. We enjoyed it, but it certainly was not a money-maker. One year, we were cutting wood and Charlie was *limbing* with Dean and got his arm in the way of the chain saw. We rushed him into the clinic in *Cloudcroft* and it took 56 stitches to get him fixed. He sure has a nice chainsaw tattoo.

When we got home with Charlie all bandaged up, we found out Chris had fallen off of stacked chairs and broke both elbows. They were sure a pair. Looked like they had been in a battle.

In 1987 Darrell wiped out on his motorcycle at 135 mph. Jane and I left our place and went to *California* to help Darrell get through rehab. We were with Darrell and GiGi about five and a half months.

Orlando Armijo kept our place alive while we were gone.

Jane and I were cutting up Mormon Tea bush to dry for tea. My knife slipped, and I cut my left index finger pretty bad. We drove out to the base dispensary to have it taken care of.

The doctor on call was not available right then and two of the on-call medics were taking care of me. They gave me a shot of Lanacane and started cleaning the wound to get the bleeding stopped.

I was sitting on the side of a gurney and had the impression that I slid off onto the floor like so much jello, but not in physical form. I started toward a dim light in the distance with a being or spirit on each side of me. We were communicating with each other without sound or sight. We just sorta floated toward that light. It was more tranquil than anything I ever experienced on earth.

A Cowboy Goes to War

We seemed to be traveling for quite some time when my fellow spirits said, "Wait ... you are not ready to go yet. You must go back."

We seemed to be going for a long time, but I was back instantly. Jane said they thought I was dead and that I had been out for about 20 minutes.

I was really in a mess. I needed clean clothes and I felt very groggy. The doctor was there and he got busy and sewed up my finger. If that is where I'm going when I die, it sure is a peaceful place. I am ready when the Lord is.

Jane and I became very restless, just couldn't settle down. We had tried coyote trapping and short-trip RV'ing. The RV'ing won out.

In August of 1991, Jane and I decided we could see a lot more of our family if we got an RV. So we sold our place and got a 35-foot fifth wheel and became fulltime RV'ers.

Epilogue
RV'ing

The term "RV'ing" has really come into its own in the last few years. We started with blanket and tarps. A few years later we added tents then sleeping bags then trailers and motor homes. Boy, what next?

After retirement we had a couple of pop-up trailers and a nice 22-foot tag-along but that wasn't enough to make us give up our home.

When the kids were all gone from home and scattered all over the country we sure got the travel bug and started looking.

We found a 35-foot 5th wheel with two slideouts. Jane and I discussed it a few days and put our place up for sale. Five days later we closed the deal on the house and two days after that on 28 August 1991, we drove off Big Jack's RV lot in *Alamogordo, New Mexico*, and were on our way.

We started learning the ropes the very first night. It was getting late by the time we got off of Big Jack's lot, so we just pulled out to the RV Family camp on *Holloman Air Force Base* to set up for the night.

The Family camp host told us to find a spot and hook up. They sure were nice because they had a water hose and chair waiting for us in this spot we picked. It was our first time to set up, so it took us awhile with "no not like that"–"like this" and so on, but we finally got it. We had just sat down to rest when an older man drove up in his RV and said, "Hey, what are you doing in my spot?" Well after some conversation and telling him how new we were he explained that when a person takes his RV to dump he leaves something to indicate that the space is taken. He was very nice and set up in the next space so we didn't have to move. We learned a lot from him.

A Cowboy Goes to War

We traded Jane's LTD in on a new 1-ton Chevy pickup. Yes it did all we asked of it but our best mileage was about 6 mpg. We were some disappointed.

On the way to *California* we stopped at *Goldwater Air Force Base* in *Gila Bend, Arizona*, to spend the night and had the honor of setting up in 104-degree temperature. Oh my we were learning and most of it the hard way!

We got set up at *Lake O'Neal* on *Camp Pendleton* and Darrell and GiGi came out to see us 'way after dark. GiGi got us a reservation at *Big Bear Lake* for the weekend and we learned a lot more. You sure do have to make wide turns on the mountain curves or you can get the trailer off the pavement and it is rough on tires. The RV spaces weren't made for that big a rig but we got in. We had a good time and saw the sights.

When we got ready to leave, we needed to dump the waste tanks so we found the RV dump station and got all positioned. When I removed the sewer cap, due to altitude differences it was really under pressure. That black water came out of there and hit me square in the chest and knocked me over backward. "Stink." GiGi was standing pretty close but she didn't get hit, but I think she is still laughing. I had to shower and change clothes but it took days for me to get rid of the smell.

We spent some time on the coast but our first RV Xmas was spent in *Deming* Sunrise RV Park.

Plans for a trip to *Alaska* were getting pretty firm, and we were adapting to fulltime RV'ing very well. We bought a book *The Milepost* which described the Alaskan Highway mile by mile, so we knew where we were the whole trip.

We got started on our *Alaska* trip about the first of May, 1992. First to Darrell and GiGi's, then North on I-5. On the 5th of May we crossed into *Canada* and spent our first night in *Hope, British Columbia.* The next morning we headed North out *of Hope, B.C.*, heading for *Dawson Creek, B.C.* That is where the Alaskan Highway starts.   That drive from *Hope* to *Dawson Creek* is beautiful canyon country with the roads carved right out of the very tall bluffs and you could see the water down in the bottom of the canyon hundreds of feet below.   Lots of green trees and lots of water.

It took us 11 days to make it to Dwayne and Vera's in *Kosalaf* on the *Kenai Peninsula* in *Alaska*.   On the way we saw bear, caribou, buffalo, fox, moose, and spent two days in a blizzard.   We drove very slow, it really wasn't very slick.   But it sure had a lot of frost heaves (asphalt bumps in the highway caused by freezing).   We didn't have any vehicle problems.

We spent the summer enjoying *Alaska*, sightseeing, fishing, being tourist.   Dwayne sure was a good cook.   Boy, could he ever make good smoked salmon, sour dough pancakes, etc.   We must have eaten a ton of fresh-picked blueberries and fresh-caught salmon and halibut.

We parked on *Seward Air Force Base* and took a cruise on *Resurrection Bay*, that was a real experience for a couple of desert rats.   We saw more seabirds and sea life than you could even think ever existed.

We lived with moose in the yard, and they were trouble.   They were not afraid of us.   We gave them the right of way.   Dwayne and Vera had about 30 sled dogs and each one had his own little dog house, which they kept straw in for bedding and the moose liked it, so they ate it.   The dogs didn't bother them at all.   And Vera never did make a fence that could keep the moose out of her garden.   There were three cow moose each with twins that visited the place pretty regular.

In August, my sisters Muriel and Nadine flew up to make the trip back with us.   After showing them around some, we headed north to *Denali National Park* and that is a story in its own right, it is fantastic.

About five days later, we headed east on a wilderness road toward *Tok, Alaska*.   We camped in gravel pits, roadside pull-offs … just wherever night found us.   Every place we stopped there seemed to be plenty of blueberries. One area that was low and wet, we drove along beside a beaver dam that must have been at least a quarter of a mile long.

One day a little early for stopping there was a picnic table beside a nice little creek, so we said why not, so we did. The next morning we were having breakfast at that picnic table and we saw a moose and her twins coming down that little stream. So I got my movie camera and started photographing them. I was on the table taking their picture and Jane, Nadine and Muriel started yelling at me. When I looked up those moose were right there, only a few feet away, but they went right on down the stream and paid no attention to me. As they passed, Nadine said, "Hey look, someone has bobbed their tails."

The next day we were driving along a thick forested area (the trees were small but very thick being so far north) and there were signs beside the road that said, "Restricted area" "Military". I hit the brakes and read the sign at the entrance gate. It was a military Arctic Survival Training Base. We turned in and with my retired ID and a military sticker on my P/U the guard on the gate just came to attention and saluted and said, "Have a good day, Major." They had a good small B.X. and commissary, so we stocked up on groceries and stuff.

Shortly after the base, we had a flat tire and my spare was low, so we traveled on slowly. The next day we came to a small house with a shop out back with an airplane beside it, so we stopped to see if we could get our tires fixed. Yes, he fixed one and aired up the other one. He was sorta in a hurry because his job was to keep track of the caribou gathering for migration. He only charged us $15 and told us where to go to get a look at the caribou gathering.

It wasn't too many miles on down the road until we came to a pull-off up on a point. Down below us there was a good-sized smooth round hill and he had said to watch that hill, and sure enough it wasn't long till a pretty good bunch of caribou came around that hill; about an hour later they came around again and the bunch was bigger. I don't remember how long we stayed there but that sure was a big bunch by the time we left. How many? Oh, several hundred.

We hit the Alaskan Highway again at *Tok, Alaska*, and headed south. On the way we followed a lake for several miles and at the south end of that lake there was a service station with information service and a spot to camp. The next morning when we got up, the mountain above was covered with Dall sheep, so we were an hour or so getting on the road because of watching the sheep.

When we got to *Dawson Creek*, we decided to go down through *Banff Provincial Park* and ended up in southern *Alberta*, so we just continued down to *Montana*. We were on a very country road with vast hay fields alongside it and the deer and antelope were sure enjoying the hay.

When we got to the *United States* border, there was a little booth beside the road with a sign on it that asked that we stop and fill out a short information card. Not a soul in sight for several miles.

At *Malmstrom Air Force Base* near *Great Falls, Montana*, we set up at the base RV park and were having supper when a thunder squall hit and was about to tear our awning off, so we were trying to roll it in, with Nadine and Muriel trying to hold it down while Jane and I were rolling it. Nadine and Muriel were so small that it kept picking them up off the ground and setting them back down. By the time we got the awning secured, we had to have another drink and reward ourselves.

We got to *Deming* all safe, sound and happy, it had been one fine trip. Jane and I then parked at Dyar and Nelda's and put in electrical service and a minimal sewer system.

This was the summer of 1992. Jane and I were still very restless so Jane, Nadine, Muriel and I took a drive up through *Hillsboro* and *Kingston* to see if we could find an RV park that we liked. Well we did, so we stopped to talk to this nice lady Delah and her stepson

Jimmy and made the proper arrangements to move up to *Kingston* in Delah's RV park called "The Buzzard's Roost".

We got moved in and set up, and Jane said, "We just need more room," so we built a 12 x 24 room adjacent to our rig which made it pretty nice. We did enjoy our stay there and we built hummingbird feeders that attracted hundreds of hummingbirds, even two pairs of the rare *Mexico* hummingbirds that are five to six inches long.

Delah's husband Buck was a master welder and he could sure make some good wine, and my specialty was making bread. Jane and Delah got to be very good friends and would go to *Truth or Consequences, New Mexico*, while I worked on our home.

About this time my health problems started getting worse. I was dizzy nearly all the time and was having stomach problems too, so we left *Kingston* for *Laughlin Air Force Base, Texas*, where they had a place to take care of military retirees. Jane's brother also lived in the area so we got to spend some time with Bill and Jean and family. Billy was one of the big shots on the *Amistad Dam* across the *Rio Grande* so we got to tour the dam.

Debby and John joined us for a few days and I went through the base clinic for a complete checkup and they said there was nothing wrong with me.

We came back as far as I-10 with Debby and John, they went on to *Hobbs* and we headed for *Las Cruces* by way of *White Sands Military Base* to go to the commissary where we stocked up on groceries. I was sure having trouble breathing.

Jane said, "We are going to the hospital! We are not leaving here until we get some answers." So I parked in the hospital parking lot and went into the clinic on emergency. They got me stabilized and said I needed to have some more tests. I said, "Okay, let me take my wife on to *Las Cruces* and get her set up and I'll come back."

The doctor said, "Major, you would never make it that far, you need attention now!"

Ralph McDougal

After an hour or so of phone calls and paperwork, the doctor said, "The best thing to do is to send you by ambulance to *Las Cruces* so you can get the care we can't give you," and he assured me that my insurance would take care of it.

"Okay, what about my wife?"

He asked, "Can she drive?"

I said, "Yes, but I'll have to get her out of the parking lot."

He said, "Like hell you will."

One of the medics said, "I can get her on the road. I was a truck driver before I became a medic."

So Jane and the medic left and he remarked, "Oh, she will be all right. You can see her as you pass her on the way in."

They put me in hospital clothes with oxygen and "a medic to monitor me" in the ambulance. We went with siren a-going but you know that Ford ambulance never did catch that Dodge and 36-foot 5th wheel!

When we got to the hospital the rig was parked in the parking lot and Jane was waiting for us in the emergency room. By this time it was dark and they had me on so many drugs that I don't remember anything till I came out of it the next afternoon and they told me I had just had a quadruple bypass.

They sure were good to me while in there and I had so much company, but I still didn't like being confined. On the 4th day after the operation I asked Dr. Hokanga how long I would have to stay in the hospital and he said, "Normally 7-10 days." I just groaned and he said, "I'll tell you what—as soon as you can walk over there (about 25 feet) and climb those four steps and come back here without help, I'll let you go home." I got up ... dragging my IV pole, I climbed those four steps, came back, sat down and said, "I'm ready." It took them two or three hours to get me ready, but I was out of there by noon.

A Cowboy Goes to War

The rig was parked at Dean's house on the street, so two or three days later I wrote out detailed instructions on how to move the rig and Dean and Darrell moved it out to the *White Sands Missile Range* RV Park. The rig needed some changing to accommodate my rehab, so we went back up to *Kingston* to get a cabinet we had left up there.

After we got the rehab under control, Jane and I borrowed a boat trailer and went to *Kingston* and got a little storage shed I had made. We (Jane, Delah & I) headed for *Carlsbad* where Debbie and John lived. That was to be a playhouse for Charlie and Kacy. We dropped Delah off at her mom's in *Roswell* and picked her up on the way back.

The next couple of years we spent time in RV parks around *Las Cruces*, sometimes at the ranch in *Deming*, a trip to Darrell and GiGi's in *California*, and in *Hobbs, New Mexico*, with John and Debbie.

All of a sudden John and Debbie retired and in their motor home started working parks all over the country. Most parks only operate during the summer so they would work wherever in the winter.

In the spring of 1995 Jane and I joined Debbie and John on the North Rim of the *Grand Canyon* and Debbie got us a spot to park in the staff area. A little later Mike, Chris, Alex and Emily joined us so we moved down to *Zion National Park* for a few days. Jane got sick so we took Alex and Emily with us and headed back to *Las Cruces* to see our doctor.

The doctor we had been seeing had left, so we saw a new doctor. Jane was getting worse all the time. The doctor said she had a liver problem but that it was not life threatening. He just needed some time to get it under control. Jane kept getting worse.

We were talking to Darrell and GiGi and they urged us to come to *California* to some good doctors, so we did. We got to their house Friday evening and GiGi called Darrell's doctor and told her the story and asked if she would come in Saturday morning to see Jane. On Saturday morning the doctor talked to Jane for a little while and made some simple tests including X-rays. When she got through she said, "I think you have cancer, but I can't be sure how bad. I want to send

Ralph McDougal

you to one of *California's* leading cancer doctors. I have called him and he has agreed to see you the first thing Monday morning. I suggest that all four of you go in together."

We were there as he opened the door. He took Jane in and checked her over real good (took about a half hour) and came back in with her and sat all four of us down and said, "There is no easy way of putting this. Jane has cancer of the spleen and it is terminal."

I asked, "What do you mean terminal?"

He said, "There is nothing anybody can do for her."

I asked, "You mean with the advances in medicine, you can't help her?"

He said, "All we can do is make her passing as comfortable as possible."

Jane didn't want to be in a hospital so Darrell and GiGi set up a bedroom for us and hospice came in with a special bed and medication with special instructions and said a nurse would be by every day to take care of Jane. Jane said, "You can come by if you want to, but I don't want you touching me. Ralph can take care of me better than you can." That lasted for a few days but as she got worse, I needed help so she agreed to let GiGi help and that was better.

Ten days after we talked to the cancer doctor, Jane passed away. We had her cremated and while waiting to get her remains, I got the 5th wheel out of storage and moved it out to *San Onofre* on the beach.

I tried RV'ing for a while and ended up back at Darrell and GiGi's.

My children all asked me to come park by them which was something to be proud of, but I guess I wasn't through traveling.

I left Darrell and GiGi's in *California* about 2:00 one morning and headed for *Oklahoma*. Why *Oklahoma*? I was in debt up to my eyeballs. I could get free RV parking for ten months to get my bills paid off. I stopped in *Deming, New Mexico* at Dyar's a couple of days and went up to *Kingston* to see Delah and Jimmy and family.

A Cowboy Goes to War

~ ~ ~

Boy, did my plans change. I brought Delah back with me and I moved up to *Kingston* and started helping her finish her Bed and Breakfast. That was in October of 1995 and we were married on January 18, 1996. We worked hard on the bed-and-breakfast but we started spending our winters down on the *Baja* in *Mexico*.

Our wedding turned out to be something very special. We planned to elope with only Rick and Beka (Delah's grandchildren), and Mike and Cleta (our friends) standing up for us, with Judge Hawkens presiding.

But that isn't the way it happened. Nadine called the evening of the 17th and asked, "What are you guys doing tomorrow?"

I said, "Delah and I are getting married."

"What time and where?"

Early in the morning of the 18th, Debbie called and we had 12 people at our wedding. After the wedding, Delah and I decided to take them all to dinner at K-Bob's Restaurant.

When we got to K-Bob's, Helen Teeter met us and asked what was going on. Delah said, "Ralph and I just got married."

Helen was a very close friend of Delah's and also the manager of K-Bob's. She hugged Delah and congratulated her. Then she said, "Just have a seat over there and give me a few minutes."

When she came back, she had set up a room and really prepared a wedding reception for us. It was so nice and a memorable wedding.

Delah and I had Jane's ashes in the rig for some time, then Dean had them for a while. There was some question by the kids and me as to what to do with them.

One day Delah asked me if Jane had ever said anything about what she would like to have done with her ashes. Well yes, when we went up the *Big Sur* she had pointed out a place she said that was so peaceful that she wouldn't mind having her ashes spread there.

Delah said, "We'll do it if that is what she wanted."

Ralph McDougal

So we got as many of the family as we could together and held a memorial service near the south end of the *Big Sur* in sight of the Hearst Castle. I think that it was appropriate for the way we had lived and to fulfill Jane's wishes.

I think this is a good place to stop. It is 2014 and Delah and I are still RV'ing and aren't ready to stay parked.

I liked to work with my hands and really would have preferred that. But when they saw that I had supervisory experience they would put me into a higher position. I couldn't refuse it because they raised my pay $2.50 an hour and it meant more money for my family. So for much of my career I had 120-140 men under me all the time, from 1957 through 1974, except for a two-year period when I built the Fixed Camera Control System ('57-66 military; '67-74 Dyna Electron, White Sands). Had a few under me before 1957, doing photo and flying. I really tried to be fair to all of my men and use the talents they had. I was the one who had to decide on who got promoted and who didn't. Some guy would have a bigger family and need the money but might not have the abilities of another one. So being completely fair with each man was always difficult. I could get things done—get the best man for the job, get the supplies and get it going. I knew enough that they couldn't snow me, and they'd sure try sometimes.

I never liked to toot my own horn. When asked why I didn't tell the details of my life sooner—that's the reason. I enjoyed my managerial positions. When you've got people working for you, first of all they've got to understand what you want them to do. Next you have to create an environment for them to do it. Then you make the supplies necessary readily available. If you give them these things— 9/10 of them will just work themselves backwards to do it. Sometimes they couldn't get the supplies they needed—or needed to make an emergency trip home. If they have a problem, you go to bat for 'em. I got a lot of chewin's—I knew my commanders pretty well.

My philosophy of life? Be fair, be honest, and if it's the truth stand up for it. If you're right—then go for it! If it takes a chewin'—it only takes five minutes!

I feel so blessed and thankful … I've had a wonderful life.

Ralph and Delah McDougal in 2013

APPENDIX
My Memoirs
Ralph Hamilton McDougal

Born: 20 February 1925 – Ft. Bayard, New Mexico

Raised: Homestead – Florida Mountains Southeast of Deming, New Mexico

Parents: Luther Hamilton (Hamp) McDougal, Mamie Frances Toney McDougal

Siblings: Alda, Nettie, Muriel, Nadine, (me), Luther, Dyar

Spouse: Vonnie Jane (Warren) McDougal

Children: Ralph Dwayne, Bruce Darrell, Deborah Lynn, William Dean, Micheal Hamp

2nd Spouse: Delah Louise (Wright) McDougal

Five Phase Career:

1) Bombardier/Navigator

2) Photography

3) Electronics – Armament & Electronics

4) Photography/Electronics

5) Retirement

1943-1946 WWII – Bombardier/Navigator

26 missions in B-26 over Europe

Combat in Martin Marauder—the 1st B-26 (During WWII there was a B-26 and an A-26. After the war the B-26s were destroyed and the A-26 became a B-26).

1947-1948 Mapped the Empire of Japan & flew reconnaissance over Korea

NCO in charge of map layout and flew as navigator.

1949-1951 Biggs Field, El Paso, Texas

Two functions: Support the Berlin Airlift, and NCO in charge of Air Police guarding planes on this end of the Berlin Airlift. When the Airlift was over, photo lab, making target maps for planes flying in the Cold War.

1951-1953 Newfoundland – Photographic Advisor to the General Staff of the Northeast Air Command

Set up Thule AFB in North Greenland – detection & early warning systems in Nord, Alert, and T3 (Ice Island). I was photographer/navigator.

1953-1957 Florida – Eglin AFB –3206 Aircraft Test Wing – Aerial Photographer

Testing new aircraft.

1957-1958 Lowry AFB, Denver, Colorado, Electronics School

1958 Malmstrom AFB, Montana, NCO in charge of Armament and Electronics

Took F-89s to William Tell to Yuma and set new records.

1959 Davis – Monthan AFB, Tucson, Arizona

Only there a short time.

1959 Kirtland AFB, Albuquerque, New Mexico F-86 Saber Jets

Straightened out the F-86 squadron, NCOIC in electronics. "Bilious the Buzzard"— squadron name – picture of buzzard with club in his hand. Straightened out electronics, ORI. Squadron disbanded.

Christmas 1959 Goose Bay AFB, Labrador, Canada

ORI – Operational Readiness Inspection

Ralph McDougal

1962 Richard Gebaur AFB, Kansas City, Missouri
Alert status for southeastern quadrant of the U.S. Panama riots.
Medical retirement.

January 1967 – December 1974
Worked for civilian contractor, Dynalectron, Electronics C-
technician to Photographic Range Supervisor.

World War II planes and other planes I was in:
B-26 Martin Marauder—the first B-26

Training: AT-11, B-17, B-24, AT-6

B-26 – flew till out of combat

F-9 (B-29), F-7 (B-17), F-2 (C-45). Modified them to handle
the photo stuff – made them an "F" instead of a "B".

Newfoundland—flew in a modified B-17 air rescue—fuel tanks
in the bomb bay – could fly 32 hours max time. Also flew C-119,
C-124, C-54, C-47, SA-16, and a DHC-2 (Beaver).

Panama riots—flew C-130, C-133, C-141.

Eglin AFB (Florida)—one I liked most was B-57, but flew in
helicopters H-5 and H-21; T-33 (jet), B-52, B-66.

There is a long list of aircraft designations, but the ones we will
be dealing with are:

A—attack plane

B—bomber

C—cargo

F—photo

T—trainer

F—fighter

RB—reconnaissance bomber

FB—fighter bomber

RF—reconnaissance fighter

Additional Books by
Patriot Media, Incorporated
Publishing America's Patriots

All books can be purchased at: **www.patriotmediainc.com** & **www.amazon.com,** with most titles available as Ebooks for Kindle Readers. Book reviews and descriptions can be seen at our web site: **www.patriotmediainc.com**.

Check the site often for discounts and special sale items.

D.M. Ulmer, Author
Silent Battleground
Shadows of Heroes
The Cold War Beneath
Ensure Plausible Deniability
Shared Glory
Skagerrak
Missing Person
The Roche Harbor Caper
The Long Beach Caper
Count the Ways
Where or When

Nelson O. Ottenhausen, Author
Civil War II
The Blue Heron
The Killing Zone
The Sin Slayer
Jugs & Bottles
The Naked Warrior
Little Hawk & Lobo

Brett Kneisley, Author
DVD-Tour of USS Clamagore

B.K. Bryans, Author
Those '67 Blues
Flight to Redemption
The Dog Robbers
Arizona Grit
Brannigan Rides Again

Joseph C. Engel, Author
Flight of the Silver Eagle

Tom Gauthier, Author
Mead's Trek
Code Name: Orion's Eye
Die Liste

Dari Bradley, Author
Hickory Nuts in the Driveway

Paul Sherbo, Author
*Unsinkable Sailors: The fall and rise of the last crew
of the Frank E. Evans*

LTC Peter Clark, Author
*Staff Monkeys: A Stockbrokers Journey through
the Global War on Terror*

Art Giberson, Author
The Mighty O

Hannah Ackerman, Author
I Kept My Chin Up

Hal Olsen, Author
Up An' Atom

Roger Chaney, Author
Carquinez Straits

A Cowboy Goes to War

Paul Stuligross, Author
The Donkey

Jack Verneski, Author
Scarecrow Season

Robert & Billie Nicholson, Authors
Pearl Harbor Honor Flight: One Last Goodbye

Ralph McDougal, Author
Mules to Missiles

Made in the USA
Coppell, TX
26 September 2024

37743748R00120